RIGHT LIVING
RIGHT GIVING

A Spiritual Journey to a Generous Lifestyle

CRAIG A. DUNN
LARRY MOORE
STAN TOLER

WESLEYAN INVESTMENT FOUNDATION

Published and Printed by Dust Jacket Press. Copyright ©2017
RIGHT LIVING, RIGHT GIVING: A Spiritual Journey to a Generous Lifestyle
Craig A. Dunn, Larry Moore & Stan Toler

ISBN: 978-0-9983908-5-7

Printed in the United States of America:
Wesleyan Investment Foundation

WIF
P. O. Box 7250
Fishers, Indiana 46037
www.wifonline.com

All Scripture quotations, unless otherwise indicated, are taken from the Holy Bible, New International Version®. NIV®. Copyright ©1973, 1978, 1984 by Biblica, Inc.® Used by permission. All rights reserved.

Scriptures marked NIV
New Living Translation (NLT), Holy Bible, New Living Translation, copyright © 1996, 2004, 2015 by Tyndale House Foundation. Used by permission of Tyndale House Publishers Inc., Carol Stream, Illinois 60188. All rights reserved.

Scriptures marked NKJV
New King James Version (NKJV), Scripture taken from the New King James Version®. Copyright © 1982 by Thomas Nelson. Used by permission. All rights reserved.

Scriptures marked KJV
King James Version (KJV),
Public Domain

Scriptures marked MSG
The Message (MSG)
Copyright © 1993, 1994, 1995, 1996, 2000, 2001, 2002 by Eugene H. Peterson

Cover and Interior Design: D.E. West / ZAQ Designs

WESLEYAN INVESTMENT FOUNDATION

TABLE OF CONTENTS

Remember: A stingy planter gets a stingy crop;
a lavish planter gets a lavish crop. I want each of you to
take plenty of time to think it over, and make up your
own mind what you will give. That will protect you
against sob stories and arm-twisting.
God loves it when the giver delights in the giving.
God can pour on the blessings in astonishing ways
so that you're ready for anything and everything, more than just
ready to do what needs to be done. As one psalmist puts it,

> *He throws caution to the winds,*
> *giving to the needy in reckless abandon.*
> *His right-living, right-giving ways*
> *never run out, never wear out.*

This most generous God who gives seed to the farmer
that becomes bread for your meals is more than extravagant
with you. He gives you something you can then give away,
which grows into full-formed lives, robust in God, wealthy
in every way, so that you can be generous in every way,
producing with us great praise to God.

2 Corinthians 9:6-11, MSG

INTRODUCTION

The challenges of right living and right giving go all the way back to Bible times. In the story of Cain and Abel, Cain's offering was given impulsively and disobediently, while Abel's was given out of love and obedience to God. The fallout was disastrous. Cain's jealousy led him to murder his brother and spend the remainder of his life as a "restless wanderer" (Genesis 4:12).

Wrong motives for doing right things often put a glitch in our daily activities. They even affect how we worship on the weekend. Trading joy for duty results in a dull emptiness. And watching others rejoice in worship can arouse feelings of resentment.

We pray that Right Living, Right Giving will be transformational. We offer you time-proven insights for living triumphantly and giving generously. And we hope these concepts will also help you in your development of a Christian worldview.

The Scriptures are highly relevant to these issues. We have personally discovered that God's directions are accompanied by the promises of His supply. They are absolute truths that contrast the world's "conditionals." And they are positive in providing spiritual security in troubled times.

In gratitude to our Lord, each of us has served His church in ministry for nearly four decades, in pastoral leadership, or financial services. And what we have learned from our on-site experiences, we delight to share with you. We believe Right Living, Right Giving will be of great value to you, as you continue to make Kingdom values a priority in your life.

Craig A. Dunn, Larry Moore & Stan Toler
2017

1

REAL FINANCIAL SECURITY

*"Trust in the Lord and do good; dwell in the land
and enjoy safe pasture" (Psalm 37:3)*

Gordon heard his pastor speak on biblical principles for giving tithes and offerings, but he wasn't buying it. Did God expect him to give blindly before he knew how the month would shake out? What assurance did he have that he could provide for the things he needed?

The words of the Psalmist provide valuable answers:

- "Trust the Lord and do good." Do what is right, in this case giving to God in obedience to His Word.

- "Dwell in the land." Rest in the security of His provision of grace.

- "Enjoy safe pasture." Trust God to resource and protect you right where you are, not just where you hope to be.

The truest financial security is trusting God with our resources and believing that He will supply what we need, when we need it. Estimating His worth is futile. Psalm 50:12b, "The world is mine, and all that is in it." Link that with Philippians 4:19, "My God will meet all your needs according to the riches of his glory in Christ Jesus." You have a spiritual portfolio that that the richest people in the world would envy.

Faith is the qualifier. God's spiritual estate is promised to His family, and the only way to become a family member is through a declared faith in Christ. John 1:12b, "To those who believed in his name, he gave the right to become children of God."

Real financial security is the knowledge that by faith, we can make spiritual withdrawals from heaven's bank in any form or amount. And that's the reason we make deposits by our living and giving in the name of our Savior.

RELATED:

"By committing the details of our lives to Him, including our finances, we acknowledge spiritually that He is a loving and trustworthy Heavenly Father." - Stan Toler

MY PRAYER:

Lord, by faith in Jesus Christ, I confess that I am a dependent and heir of heaven's riches. Help me to live as an obedient child in Your heavenly family. Amen.

2

SAFE FROM RECESSION

*"For Where your treasure is, there your heart
will be also" (Matthew 6:21)*

Ask someone who lost nearly everything in the Recession of 2008 about treasure. They may tell you that it is unwise, even disastrous, to focus your identity and worth only on what it is in your 401k or pension account. There are simply too many economic blips. Wouldn't it be wiser to invest in something that has unlimited funding and has only grown in value from the beginning of time?

Jesus gave us investment advice centuries ago that is just as relevant as the latest column on a financial website. Addressing thousands from varied classes and incomes in an illustration during His Sermon on the Mount. He told them to store their treasure in heaven.

You know the axiom, "one person's trash is another person's treasure." The fact is, another person's treasure may not even be treasured by others. One may be thinking about earthly treasure, and the other heavenly. One is seen, the other unseen. One has an estimated value, the other a guaranteed. One may be stolen, and the other is secure. One may be subject to recession, while the other is recession-proof.

Living a Spirit-filled, Spirit-directed life means listening for His "stops" and "starts." It's a life that aligns itself with the whole or "pop-ups" of God's Word. The Bible says "Do not love this world nor the things it offers you, for when you love the world, you do not have the love of the Father in you" (1 John 2:15, NLT).

If that sounds radical, it is! Whatever we treasure more than God's approval topples Him from the throne of our heart. So, if we trust earth more than heaven, we're more earthly than heavenly. If we bank only on the systems of this world, we neglect the most recession-proof investment there is: investing in the eternal.

Invest in the eternal. It will be secure. And your heart will follow.

RELATED:

"Only one life, 'twill soon be past; only what's done for Christ will last." – A.B. Simpson

MY PRAYER:

Lord, search my heart for the things that increasingly draw my attention away from the eternal. Amen.

~~~~~~

3

EVERYTHING IS A GIFT

"The earth is the Lord's, and everything in it, the world and
all who live in it" (Psalm 24:1)

Shelly poured milk over the cereal in her preschooler's bowl and wondered again how she had been lucky enough to become a mom. After years of infertility, the birth of their daughter had been a dream come true for Shelly and her husband, Jim. Putting the milk back in the fridge, she saw the door magnet which said "Blessings come in many ways" and stopped. Yes, little Alyssa Dawn was a blessing. Maybe it hadn't been luck, but rather the good hand of God which had given her the gift of motherhood.

Like Shelly, we need to recognize God's gifts in our everyday lives. Seeing our community and homes, and the people in them, as coming from Him, and belonging to Him, changes our perspective. Some see their blessings as self-produced. "Self-made millionaire" may be a dated term to some, but Google it and you'll find over millions of pages devoted to describing one, or instructions on how to become one.

The Old Testament book of Job has an interesting dialogue between the man who lost everything and the One who created everything. In Job 38, Creator God asks some mind-blowing questions:

- "Where were you when I laid the earth's foundation? Tell me, if you understand."

- "Have you comprehended the vast expanses of the earth?"

- "Who provides food for the raven?"

What we have, and what we give, comes from the belief in the One who is constantly blessing us with them. Counting our blessings doesn't mean compiling an inventory or arranging an appraisal of our stuff. It means treasuring God's goodness in our heart, being grateful for His unexpected gifts, and purposefully giving Him our thanks.

RELATED:
"The American Dream makes it seem as if our wealth comes from our determination, hard work, and free-spirited entrepreneurship (and all these things are good), but God is the true source." - Craig Dunn

MY PRAYER:
Father, help me to aim for success with the understanding that everything I have was Yours from the beginning. Amen.

〜〜〜〜〜〜〜〜〜〜〜〜〜〜〜〜〜〜〜〜〜〜〜〜〜〜〜〜〜

4

HE WILL CARRY YOU

"The Lord your God, who is going before you, will fight for you, as he did for you in Egypt. There you saw how the Lord your God carried you, as a father carries his son" (Deuteronomy 1:30a-31b)

There is something heartwarming about seeing a parent with a baby strapped to their chest or back. God reminded the nation of Israel of His faithful fatherhood by reminiscing that He had "carried them" all the way through the wilderness. When they were tired and hungry, and about to give up, He picked them up and brought them through.

Carrying a baby has advantages both for you and for the baby. For you, it gives you a sense of providing and protecting, which in turn gives the baby a sense of security. God loves to take care of you! The Scripture says "I am convinced that nothing can ever separate us from God's love" (Romans 8:39, NLT).

As His child, that "faith fact" of His never-ending love is a source of assurance, comfort, and affirmation. From earliest childhood, most of us have sung, "Jesus loves me this I know, for the Bible tells me so; little ones to Him belong, they are weak but He is strong." Rest for your weariness. Food for your hunger. Courage for your weakness. The way God takes care of you exceeds every earthly model of caring.

He is faithful to those called by His name. Whatever wilderness you are facing, you can count on Him. And that love calls us to action; it calls us to express it in very real ways. We love and serve Him because He loves and serves us. Faithfulness is our best response to the faithfulness of God.

RELATED:

"Human love is controlled by human emotions that ebb and flow with life's changing tides. God's love is constant and unstoppable." – Larry Moore

MY PRAYER:

Father, give me a faith that proves itself by its expressions and actions of love, first to You, and then to others. Amen.

5

GOD IS NOT A SCROOGE

*"Every good and perfect gift is from above, coming down
from the Father of the heavenly lights, who does not
change like shifting shadows" (James 1:17)*

The name Ebenezer Scrooge is synonymous with stin-
giness. God's name is synonymous with generosity.
Scrooge was the miser of all misers. God is the Giver who out-
gives all givers. To even mention the fictitious Scrooge character
in the same breath as that of a living God seems sacrilegious. But
it is mentioned to dispel the bad rap He often gets when things
don't go our way.

A hurricane floods a community, leaving muddy ruin. Tor-
nadoes leapfrog through a neighborhood, leaving some homes in-
tact while others are reduced to stacks of shattered lumber. God's
reputation is often reduced to a clause in the insurance policy,
titled, "Acts of God."

Maybe we ought to look at a pastel sunrise or golden sunset,
and say, "Now, that's a real act of God!" Granted, He can use

adversity to accomplish His redemptive purpose, but even His justice is as loving and pure as His compassion.

Think of what you have today because of Him. Everything good in your life is from Him. The Psalmist must have had a WOW! moment when he wrote, "I say to the Lord, 'You are my Lord; apart from you I have no good thing'" (Psalm 16:2). That doesn't sound like a Scrooge, does it?

And all God asks in return is to be a wise and generous manager of the resources He has given us. Spiritual blessings. Material blessings. Relational blessings. His favor is seen everywhere.

RELATED:

"Sharing a blessing is like sharing the flame on a candle; it spreads the light. When you share good things God has given, you increase the blessing. It never diminishes." - Stan Toler

MY PRAYER:

Jesus, when I think of You, I think of the greatest blessing God has ever given. Your example lights my journey. And Your mission becomes mine, not just because of what You've done for me, but also because of what You want to do for others through me. Amen.

6

USE THE RIGHT THEOREM

"But seek first his kingdom and his righteousness, and all these things will be given to you as well" (Matthew 6:33)

Just as the mathematical science of geometry is built on certain axioms and theorems, the kingdom of God has foundational principles that influence every area of life. Focusing on knowing God, and bringing Him glory, certifies our dependence on Him for all we need to live out the lives He planned for us.

The matter of having right priorities simply means putting the most important theorem into practice first, and then all the other factors fall into place. Many start developing fresh priorities at the beginning of a new year. They dust off their One-Year Bible. They sign up for the special discount at the fitness center. They fine-tune their resolutions; adding more and then erasing, or making mental exemptions.

Others start at the first of the week. After all, they get 52 tries each year to get their weekly ducks in a row. And of course, they make spiritual vows for the worship time at church, declaring their participation in the "week of witness" or the 24-hour fast. They even bring their tithe envelope to church or give online, intent on obeying God's instructions to "Bring the whole tithe into the storehouse, that there may be food in my house" (Malachi 3:10a).

But the yearly, monthly or weekly surge won't happen without the daily steps. Faith is a walk, not a leap. Seeking the kingdom and righteousness is a daily priority. Daily obedience in living or giving provides the stamina for the weeks, months, and years ahead.

RELATED:

"As followers of Christ, we really have no other option than to give ourselves to His cause willingly and generously." – Jo Anne Lyon

MY PRAYER:

Lord Jesus, help me to understand that when I pledge to give You my day, I am actually giving You my life. Help me to understand that minutes and hours and days are gifts of Your hand, and that I am their investor on Your behalf. Amen.

7

A SURE-FIRE INVESTMENT

"A wicked person earns deceptive wages, but the one who sows righteousness reaps a sure reward" (Proverbs 11:18)

"Have I got a deal for You!" someone may say, and you'll probably think to yourself, "That's probably as much a question as it is an exclamation." So-called "good deals" are as abundant as advertising flyers on a grocery store bulletin board. But when someone spells out the deal in writing and backs it by their wisdom and experience, it might be worth a second look.

Financial counselors don't have a file for this type of account. But God tells us to invest our life's resources in "righteousness." "Wait!" you may caution, "Righteousness isn't for sale." And you're right. Being "right with God" isn't up for bids. The price has already been paid. First John 1:9, "If we confess our sins, he is faithful and just and will forgive us our sins and purify us from all unrighteousness." That's not just a "good deal," it's a "Great deal!" offered by God, guaranteed in writing, and is backed by His eternal wisdom and resource.

When you accept His "deal" by putting your faith in Christ, you begin a new life of giving Him everything you have, as well as everything you are. Your daily gifts of obedience, service, holy living, and generosity are "investments" in God's kingdom.

The most "sure-fire" investment you will ever make is to invest your time, talent, and treasure in being what He asks you to be, doing what He asks you to do, going where He asks you to go, and giving what He asks you to give. The earnings on that investment accrue until your buyout is celebrated in heaven.

RELATED:

"God has given us two hands, one to receive with and the others to give with. We are not cisterns made for hoarding; we are channels made for sharing." - Billy Graham

MY PRAYER:

Lord, thank You for making such an enormous investment in my life through the death and resurrection of Jesus Christ. From a heart of thanksgiving, I pledge the investment of my life in the advancement of Your kingdom. Amen.

~~~~~~

8

IT'S TIME TO GIVE

"There is a time for everything, and a season for every activity under the heavens" (Ecclesiastes 3:1)

Grant looked at the numbers on the monitor and was amazed. Each time he checked the balance on his bank account, he felt anxious. There was always just a little more expense than he had planned.

But last week he determined to follow God's Word and to engage in regular giving to the Lord through his local church. He was praying for wisdom to budget correctly. And he knew there was no better time than the present to obey. Now, he just couldn't believe what he was seeing. God was making it work!

We are a people created for the seasons. The stream of God's wisdom flows accordingly through the spring, summer, fall, and winter of our lives. Our physical and emotional conditions are subject to changes in the light and the weather. For some, those changing conditions make such an impact that they create seasonal disorders. For others, each season brings new discoveries.

We also experience spiritual seasons. Biblical history highlights seasons of revival or complacency, growth or loss, prosperity or poverty. Only one spiritual season is continual. It's God's season of spiritual restoration and new life. The Bible says "I tell you, now is the time of God's favor, now is the day of salvation" (2 Corinthians 6:2b).

Obedience in managing God's resources is a step of growth and revival. James the apostle wrote, "Come near to God and he will come near to you" (James 4:8a). It is always time to draw near to God, no matter in what season we find ourselves. And with the drawing near, He gives us appropriate insight from His storehouse of wisdom.

RELATED:

"Out of His abundance and love, God poured out His supply, giving us what we could not earn or buy." - Craig Dunn

MY PRAYER:

Lord of the universe, my time is in Your hands. And Your all-wise timing supplies what I need just when I need it. Make me sensitive to respond to You in a timely manner. Amen.

~~~~~~

9

LIKE A PARENT GIVES

"If you then, though you are evil, know how to give good gifts to your children, how much more will your Father in heaven give the Holy Spirit to those who ask him!" (Luke 11:13)

Ella had to smile at the look of pure joy on the face of her little boy. It was worth all the hours spent passing bags of hamburgers and fries out a little window in freezing weather. She'd gladly work overtime in that fast-food restaurant to have the privilege of providing for her children.

Things had been hard since her husband had decided his life goals lay elsewhere, and walked out. Ella had struggled to keep her little family afloat. But God had provided her with both extra income and extra work, and she was glad for both. Now she could care for her children's needs.

Scores of people who excelled in their profession point to parents whose outpouring of love and support affirmed them. The dictionary defines "parent" as someone who births and nurtures a child. The psalmist portrayed the Heavenly Father in a tender and nurturing way, "The Lord is like a father to his children, tender and compassionate" (Psalm 103:13a, NLT).

So, when Jesus taught His disciples about the importance of praying in the Spirit, He naturally referred to His Heavenly Father's generosity. "How much more will your Father in heaven give the Holy Spirit to those who ask."

Christ followers are generous and compassionate. Their love for God compels them to respond in love to the concerns of His kingdom, like a parent gives. This point of surrender from a heart of love is at the core of Christian living. We love because His love was outpoured on us. We give because He gave. And we give, not out of blind allegiance, but out of enlightened trust.

RELATED:

"If you are going to trust totally, you must come to the point of acting on what you believe." - Larry Moore

---

MY PRAYER:

Father, the outpouring of Your compassion and generosity both draws me to You and inspires me to be like You. May I learn to give "as a parent."

~~~~~~

10

WHATEVER YOU NEED

*"Praise be to the God and Father of our Lord Jesus Christ,
who has blessed us in the heavenly realms with every
spiritual blessing in Christ" (Ephesians 1:3)*

"Dad, do you want me to pack this lantern?" "Absolutely, Son. We'll certainly need it on this camping trip."

Steve pulled the cord tight on his sleeping bag before he tossed it into the back of his pickup, then turned to his eight-year-old, "Let's get the rest of this stuff loaded, and then we'll head to the outfitters."

"What's that?"

"It's a place where you buy provisions, stuff you'll need to survive in the woods." His son's heart beat a little faster in anticipation. He was planning this trip for a long time, and he could almost smell the campfire aroma and the hot dogs cooking over the flame.

Your heavenly Father has been planning your trip to heaven since before time. And He isn't about to let you set up your campsites on earth without provisions. There's a line from a favorite hymn that ought to play over and over in our hearts, "All I have needed Thy hand hath provided; great is Thy faithfulness, Lord unto me."

Sometimes followers of Jesus get to take the "scenic route." You know, the one with the winding road, long miles, and unexpected breakdowns. Maybe you've experienced a flat tire or two, and your vehicle was so loaded you couldn't get to the spare. Then you remembered that road service came with your auto insurance policy! You never needed it 'til then, but you were glad you had it.

God has provisions for your trip, even emergency provisions. His supply is so great that He not only provides for the moment, He gives enough extra for you to supply others, and enough to acknowledge it by giving back a percentage of His money.

RELATED:

"God doesn't give us everything we want, but He gives us everything we need." - Unknown

MY PRAYER:

Father, thank You for providing everything I need through Jesus Christ for my journey to heaven. I am blessed beyond measure to be Your child. Amen.

~~~~~~~~~~~~~~~~~~~~~~~~~~~~~~~~

11

FAITHFUL ALWAYS

*"His master replied, 'Well done, good and faithful servant!
You have been faithful with a few things; I will put you
in charge of many things. Come and share your master's
happiness!'" (Matthew 25:21)*

Over 600 crew members perished on the maiden voyage
of the infamous Titanic. Many of those bore the title of
steward. They gave their lives in serving the passengers, cleaning
staterooms, distributing meals, and performing other duties on
board ship.

The dictionary defines "steward" as one who manages the
affairs of another. Scripturally, stewards faithfully manage the
resources of God's kingdom. But interestingly, they do that by
managing their own, God-given resources.

In Jesus' parable, the master's happiness with the servant's
work is linked to the servant's faithful management. It's a practical
application of Luke 12:48b, "From everyone who has been given
much, much will be demanded."

Stewardship is a full-orbed principle of faithfully serving Christ in what He has given to us to do, using the skills He gave us, and completing it within the time allotted for us. James the apostle highlighted the principle, and added the component of faith: "Someone will say, 'You have faith; I have deeds.' Show me your faith without deeds, and I will show you my faith by my deeds" (James 2:18). In other words, the belief of faith without the employment of faith in service to God and others is an idle belief. We show faith by how we live, what we do, and what we give.

Everything belongs to God in the first place. So, everything we have is on loan from Him, subject to our careful use, and rewarded by His trusting us with other things.

RELATED:

"You and I are called to offer what we have to Jesus so that He might bless it, and extend it to others." - Stan Toler

MY PRAYER:

Lord Jesus, I pledge to follow You with all that I have and all that I am. Strengthen me to be a faithful steward-manager in the place where You have appointed me, in the time you have given me. Amen.

1 2

SOW WITH A FULL HAND

*"Remember this: Whoever sows sparingly will also reap
sparingly, and whoever sows generously will also reap generously"
(2 Corinthians 9:6)*

Jason is a farmer in Indiana whose land has been passed
down through four generations. His family has spent their
life working the land, planting and harvesting crops, row after
row. And they always plant as generously as possible. With today's farm machinery, it's easier to plant even, full rows. But in
the past, when his great-grandparents forged this homestead with
hours of sweat and hard work, the planting was a painstaking process. Prized seeds were hand-tossed or planted one at a time into
the soil.

Jason will always remember his Granddad saying "Sowing
is like giving to God; do it with a full hand." Handfuls of seed
planted mean a greater amount harvested. It's a spiritual law: "sow
generously, reap generously."

Amazingly, some still debate whether their giving percentage should be based on gross income or net. But the principle stands: If you sow with a handful of seed you will reap a greater harvest.

A giving competition with Jesus would be an exercise in futility. Who could ever out-give the One who willingly sacrificed His own life for our sin! And all He demands in return is for us to respond generously, and He responds from His eternal supply line.

Probably from childhood you have heard that a "penny saved is a penny earned." That's a sound financial principle, but in the economy of the Kingdom, we might offer a different take on it. Of course, the stewardship of God's resources means practicing sound money principles, including saving pennies and debt reduction. But we must always remember who owns the penny! And remember that its Heavenly Owner has the final word on its saving or giving: sow generously.

RELATED:

"The reality is that God knows each of us and gives us the things that we can most effectively use in His service." – Dan Schafer

MY PRAYER:

Father, may I always sow with a full hand, believing that abundant giving is the result of the abundant living You have made possible. Amen.

~~~~~~

13

REAPING JOYFULLY

"Still other seed fell on good soil, where it produced a crop—a hundred, sixty or thirty times what was sown" (Matthew 13:8)

Tracy looked out her kitchen window and smiled. The zinnias had really taken hold in the soft ground of the backyard. Those dried petals she had saved so carefully were now wonderfully multiplied, in red, purple, yellow, and orange glory. It was so amazing, that dormant spark of life dozing inside a tiny seed. Given the right conditions, it would burst forth, and her crop of flowers was proof.

She sat down at the kitchen table and pulled her Bible closer, remembering Jesus' words about reaping a crop from good soil and thinking about how that principle had been demonstrated in her own life. She had reaped so much from investing her heart and strength in His kingdom.

Sometimes it seems that there are more causes than there are diseases or disasters, each with its own website or marathon run. Deciding which to support, is as much about the heart as it is its visual or emotional appeal. Christ-followers, of all people, should have a heart of compassion for the needs of others, and participate as much as possible.

But where does giving for earthly causes stand in comparison to investing in the heavenly Kingdom? That's an important question. And one that goes to the very soul of our consecration. Causes come and go with new discoveries or treatments. Pop causes run their course; Kingdom causes are eternal.

So, the question is in what "soil" do we plant the seed? That depends on its eternal value. Plant it in the temporal, and it will bring a temporal gain. Plant it in the eternal, and it will be multiplied eternally. We really will reap what we sow.

RELATED:

"What can you do today to make it possible for someone else to draw near to God?" –Melvin Maxwell

MY PRAYER:

Lord, make me sensitive to the leadings of Your Holy Spirit in my living and giving. Help me to always be grateful for what I have reaped from You. Amen.

1 4

EXERCISE YOUR GIVING

"But since you excel in everything—in faith, in speech,
in knowledge, in complete earnestness and in the love we
have kindled in you—see that you also excel in this grace of giving"
(2 Corinthians 8:7)

We spend nearly $50-billion each year on fitness products. Exercise videos fill the airwaves. Fitness centers sprout up in towns of nearly every size. Entrepreneurs devise new ways to sell old ideas in fitness equipment.

Considering our bodies are a "temple of the Holy Spirit," physical fitness certainly has its place. But there's an interesting guideline in God's Word: "Physical training is of some value, but godliness has value for all things, holding promise for both the present life and the life to come" (1 Timothy 4:8).

You may start your day with an exercise routine that incorporates cardio and strength training, but have you ever considered starting your week with an exercise in giving? The early church did. They practiced the giving of their tithe (the tenth), "On the first day of every week, each one of you should set aside a sum of money in keeping with your income" (1 Corinthians 16:2a). And they gave faithfully for the needs of the church. Acts 4:32b, "No one claimed that any of their possessions was their own, but they shared everything they had."

Exercise giving? How? Here are a few suggestions:

- Stretching - by increasing your gifts.
- Weightlifting - by lifting the weight off someone's shoulders through volunteering.
- Deep knee bends - by praying for the staff of the ministries you support.
- Running - by setting the pace for promoting and supporting ministry projects.
- Chin-ups - by being joyful in service, and rising above negative thoughts about giving.

"See that you also excel in this grace of giving" (2 Corinthians 8:7)

RELATED:

"Obedience in giving adds to our spiritual wealth. We become wealthier in faith, more apt to trust God for added blessing and to become richer in influence." –Brian Kluth

MY PRAYER:

Dear Jesus, help me to always be concerned about my spiritual fitness, and to exercise the grace of giving. Amen.

~~~~~~~~~~~~~~~~~~~~~~~~~~~~~~

1 5

AN ANCESTRY TO CHERISH

"In you our ancestors put their trust; they trusted and you delivered them. To you they cried out and were saved; in you they trusted and were not put to shame" (Psalm 22:4-5).

There are 75 million searches daily on Ancestry.com. This huge database has helped millions connect with their past. Researchers often uncover astonishing facts about those who lived before them, sometimes good, sometimes not.

The people of Israel have an incredible history. The biblical record recounts God's wonders displayed on their behalf. Over and over He provided resources for them in amazing ways and various situations, during years of captivity, marching in the wilderness, standing before the Red Sea, or facing warring tribal nations. His resources on their behalf were limitless.

The songwriter expressed the wealth of those resources, "His love has no limit, His grace has no measure, His power has no boundary known unto men." We come to God with confidence, no matter our physical, spiritual, emotional, or financial need. None will exhaust His supply, and none will threaten His kingdom.

Right living in a world gone wrong? No problem. What an ancestry we have! He brought Noah through the flood. He brought Daniel through the fire. He also brought David out of a pit of guilt, brought Peter through the shame of betrayal, and brought Rahab out of a brothel. Modern times are filled with equally miraculous salvation stories that never make the nightly news. Our ancestry is proof of God's awesome resources.

You may have every piece of your faith together except the giving part. You may have surrendered everything to God but the checkbook. Guess what? He wants you more than your checkbook. And you need Him more than anything else. Once that part of the relationship is healed, both your giving and receiving will fall into place.

RELATED:

"What size is the spiritual container you'll use to dip into God's supply? It needs to be faith-sized." –Mark Hollingsworth

MY PRAYER:

Creator God, thank You for being the Eternal Source. And thank You for a family relationship with You that is dependable and loving. Amen.

16

IT MEANS A TENTH

"Bring the whole tithe into the storehouse, that there may be food in my house. Test me in this," says the Lord Almighty, "and see if I will not throw open the floodgates of heaven and pour out so much blessing that there will not be room enough to store it" (Malachi 3:10)

"Dad, will you help me with my math homework? It's fractions!"

Glenn wanted to groan, but he put down the remote, slid out of his lounge chair, and slowly walked to the dining room. His fourth-grade son sat at the table, squinting at a sheet of paper.

"Fractions, huh? This stuff will really help you in life!"

Tyler looked skeptical. "You sound like my teacher. Is that because you're a pastor?"

Glenn smiled. "Could be. And because I am a pastor, I know that fractions even help people live according to the Bible."

"Really?"

"Yes, son. You heard me speak about tithing last Sunday. Well, did you know that the word tithe actually means "a tenth?"

Tithing, giving a tenth of our increase back to God, may not be called the "Golden Rule" in Scripture, but it certainly gives us a clearly defined instruction on how to rule the gold. Money in the hands of people who live by humanistic principles causes more grief than gain. First Timothy 6:10, "The love of money is a root of all kinds of evil. Some people, eager for money, have wandered from the faith and pierced themselves with many griefs."

Every command of God has our good in mind, including giving our tithes. God's principle of the tenth provides a fair and equitable way for every believer to invest in His eternal kingdom, and at the same time, invest in their spiritual and physical welfare.

RELATED:

"The gift of 10% has precedence all the way back to the time of Abraham. Tithing is a guide to giving for today's Christian."
- Wayne Watts

MY PRAYER:

Father, help me to understand that giving the Tenth to You benefits me as a person more than it benefits You as a provider. Amen.

1 7

THANKFULNESS AND STEWARDSHIP

*"Give thanks to the Lord, for he is good. His love
endures forever" (Psalm 136:1)*

Drive through the neighborhoods of your town, and observe the curbside appearance of the properties. Chances are you'll see various levels of maintenance, whether the neighborhood is affluent or not.

Sometimes, there are circumstances beyond the control of the owners which affect the conditions of their properties, but to a great measure, property conditions reflect the commitment of their managers. Those to whom life is a lark and possessions are "easy come, easy go," often lack an appreciation for what they have and the investment it took them (or maybe others) to get it.

One banking website suggests it takes over $2-thousand per year to maintain the average home. Another says yearly maintenance costs equal one percent of the home's purchase price. No matter which is accurate, we know it takes dollars to make a property look pricey.

Christ-followers understand homeowners are simply managers-in-residence. Legally, what they have is on their balance sheet, but spiritually it all belongs to the One who gave it to them.

Gratitude is a key component in right living and right giving. Every step we take, we take over the ground God formed and parceled out to us. We've witnessed scenes of someone departing an airplane, and reaching the end of its stairway, kneeling and kissing the ground. They aren't worshipping the earth - they're acknowledging the gift of freedom, or arrival, or even comparison to other environments.

"Give thanks to the Lord." What a simple request for the abundance He has provided. James 1:17, "Every good and perfect gift is from above." Our gratitude acknowledges it, and our giving proves it.

Then, when you add "His love endures forever," you see that His giving and ours is linked in abiding love. As a Father, He gives in love. And as a child, we receive in love and give gratefully.

RELATED:

"Every act of alignment with the Father's will results in ultimate blessing." –Tom Hermiz

MY PRAYER:

Lord, I acknowledge that my gifts to You could never express my love for You, or Your love for me. But I give them in obedience and thankfulness. Amen.

1 8

WISE WORSHIP

*"Now faith is confidence in what we hope for and assurance
about what we do not see. This is what the ancients were
commended for" (Hebrews 11:1-2)*

One of the most beautiful worship services in history took place in the humblest circumstances. "After Jesus was born in Bethlehem in Judea, during the time of King Herod, Magi from the east came to Jerusalem and asked, "Where is the one who has been born king of the Jews? We saw his star when it rose and have come to worship him" (Matthew 2:1-2).

We're told the names of the wise men from Arabia, Persia, and India who visited the Christ Child were Balthasar, Melchior, and Gaspar. They were drawn to someone who they hoped would give them what they lacked in their heart. Matthew tells us how their worship unfolded.

We see four important lessons in Matthew 2:

First, their worship teaches us that God is always drawing us, and it always ends with Jesus. "The star they had seen when it rose went ahead of them until it stopped over the place where the child was." (V. 9).

Second, their worship teaches us that acknowledging Christ's lordship is at the very heart of Christian living and giving. "They saw the child with his mother Mary, and they bowed down and worshiped him." (V. 11a).

Third, their worship teaches us that Jesus deserves the very best we can offer Him. "They opened their treasures and presented him with gifts of gold, frankincense, and myrrh." (V. 11b).

Fourth, their worship teaches us that God's approval is worth more than man's opinion. "Warned in a dream not to go back to Herod, they returned to their country by another route." (V. 12).

God turned a humble moment into a magnificent moment of grace and truth. He always does that when we surrender what we have for what we cannot see.

RELATED:

"We need to present God with the first and the best." –Norman Wilson

MY PRAYER:

Lord, thank you for drawing me to Yourself and then accepting who I am and what I have as an offering of my love. Amen.

19

HOW TO GROW YOUR FUTURE

*"Commit your way to the Lord; trust in him
and he will do this" (Psalm 37:5)*

Studies show that 1 in 3 Americans has saved nothing for retirement. We are a "now" culture, spending our tomorrows today, forking over ever increasing sums of money to pay for needs and wants. And often using the "plastic" of credit instead of "gold" resources in the process.

How can one grow a nest egg in such conditions?

By committing our way to the Lord, we align ourselves with the economy of God's kingdom. That economy focuses more on eternal investment than immediate spending. Jesus promised daily bread provisions, but He also promised an eternal return on what we invest in His kingdom.

No, heaven doesn't send us stock reports or financial statements. We invest visible resources in an unseen Kingdom. And just as we trusted the Lord for our salvation and sanctification, we trust Him for our eternal provision. "This is accomplished from start to finish by faith. As the Scriptures say, 'It is through faith that a righteous person has life.'" (Romans 1:17 NLT).

Interestingly, we grow our future by surrendering our past and present to Christ. In some ways that is like opening an account in "Heaven's Savings and Loan." Led by the Holy Spirit, we make deposits of time, talent, or treasure, and those deposits accrue over time. We could also use the analogy that what we invest in the Kingdom is also used to meet the needs of Kingdom interests.

Like no other investment, when we make deposits in the Kingdom of God, they are covered by the unlimited assets of the Creator and Provider.

Grow your future now. Invest with love and obedience in the Kingdom of Heaven.

RELATED:

"Stewardship is partnering with God in His great plan to reconcile the world to Himself." –Steve Weber

MY PRAYER:

Heavenly Father, I acknowledge that You are the Creator and Provider who has committed heaven's riches in Christ Jesus to me. In return, I covenant to invest my resources in Your kingdom. Amen.

20

DIVIDED FOCUS

"No one can serve two masters. Either you will hate the one and love the other, or you will be devoted to the one and despise the other. You cannot serve both God and money" (Matthew 6:24)

An article published in USNews.com claimed that out of three thousand people surveyed, more than 1 in 3 have a "moonlight" job; an additional source of employment to supplement their income. Moonlighting is a common practice that either gives people more "gravy" or sends them to an early grave.

With the rising cost of living and our western appetite for more, many take an extra job just to survive. Some succeed in dealing with the extra workload and time restraints of moonlighting, but many find it difficult to totally give their best efforts to one line of work while dabbling in another.

There is only so much energy to use and only so many hours in the day, not to mention only so much mental focus. And while many work two jobs they hate, some find more fulfillment in one over the other. It is a divided focus.

Jesus warned, "No one can serve two masters." Right living demands undivided spiritual focus. We can't keep our eyes on the finish line and window shop in the world at the same time.

Temptation is the devil's modus operandi; he's always working on setting window displays. He was brazen enough to show Jesus a "PowerPoint presentation" of the earth, and guarantee Him ownership in return for His allegiance. But Jesus resisted with a Scripture and a boot!

If we're not careful, the very things that seem to be wise investments of our time, talent, or treasure, can quickly become losses on our spiritual balance sheet.

Choose God over money, and money will become your servant rather than your master.

RELATED:

"When we learn to be content with what He has given us, we will realize that there is no satisfaction like the fullness God can provide." – Dorothy Meadows

MY PRAYER:

Jesus, I choose to focus on You rather than on the stuff of this earth. Amen.

～～～～～～～～～～～～～～～～～～～～～

2 1

INVEST YOUR HEART

"For where your treasure is, there your heart
will be also" (Luke 12:34)

Joe pulled out of the hospital parking lot. He had been crying. He wanted to hide it from the staff, and even from his wife for whom he wanted to stay strong, but to no avail. You don't leave your five-year-old daughter, the exuberant, pony-tailed joy of your life in a pediatric unit and go off to work as usual.

His heart was on the 12th floor of the hospital. And he would do whatever necessary, and spend his last dollar to get her well. Jesus knows that where our hearts are invested, our treasure is found. His greatest sacrifice proved it. "It is finished," were His last words from the cross where He had invested His life for everyone on earth. It was an everlasting love that was restless until it finished its mission.

John wrote of Christ's love for His disciples, "Jesus knew that the hour had come for him to leave this world and go to the Father. Having loved his own who were in the world, he loved them to the end" (John 13:1b).

"Put your heart in it" are the familiar words of every coach or mentor. They know that the value people attribute to something determines what they give to it. Looking back over a lost game, a coach may lament, "They lost heart." Christian faith is an agreement of head and heart. But faith made just of head knowledge without heart, seldom crosses the finish line.

Do you have a heart for giving? If not, it's time to check your connection. It could be a matter of being unplugged to the source of joy, the triumphant and joyous Savior.

RELATED:

"Sacrifices offered to the Lord rise before Him as a pleasant aroma. Giving bears the scent of heaven's kind of love." – Jo Anne Lyon

MY PRAYER:

Lord, give me a new heart of joy for serving You in Your mission. Let the sacrifice You showed at Calvary be my standard for living and giving. Amen.

2 2

SO MANY THINGS TO LOVE

"Do not love the world or anything in the world. If anyone loves the world, love for the Father is not in them. The world and its desires pass away, but whoever does the will of God lives forever" (1 John 2:15,17)

The word "love" is overused. We all know it. We "love" everything from our family to TV shows to sports teams to cars to food to coffee.

A popular website listed things people "love:"

- Baby animals
- Beaches
- Josh Groban
- Dinosaurs
- Festivals
- Flowers
- Noodles
- Social media
- Sports

There was a total of 30 items on the list. That's a lot of love floating around, but it's mostly focused on the things in this present world, not the one to come. And to those things that we pledge our allegiance, we also make investments of time and money.

Scriptures tell us to love heaven more than earth. To "lift up [our] heads, because [our] redemption is drawing near" (Luke 21:28b, emphasis added). In other words, love the finish line, rather than the race course.

Earthly stuff is easier to prize; we are likely to be drawn to what's seen. For example, bank statements are more visible than eternal treasures. Real estate can be appraised, while a heavenly home can only be imagined. And the greatest treasure we have also is based on what we can't see: our relationship with Jesus. "Though you have not seen him, you love him; and even though you do not see him now, you believe in him and are filled with an inexpressible and glorious joy" (1 Peter 1:8). What's burning in your heart, or puts a gleam in your eye? May your love for Jesus and His kingdom motivate your life's investment.

RELATED:

"Man needs a total God to serve Him fully in this present world, and in turn, God demands a total man as a channel for redemption's power running into every area of human life." - Samuel Young

MY PRAYER:

Lord Jesus, You are my first love, more important than anything or anyone on earth. And I treasure our relationship. Amen.

23

OBEDIENCE IS LOVE

"Whoever has my commands and keeps them is the one who loves me. The one who loves me will be loved by my Father, and I too will love them and show myself to them" (John 14:21).

"God loves (cares for, cherishes) me as I am." True. "God accepts (affirms) me as I am." True. "God approves (tolerates) everything I do." False.

Many equate a relationship with God as universal acceptance and tolerance, passive interaction on His part. But in fact, Jesus told us that our loving relationship with Him is shown by our obedience, by active interaction on our part.

Similar to the love in human relationships, a relationship with the divine has boundaries and responsibilities. However, since God is both our Creator and Lord, our relationship with Him also includes obedience to His authority. This principle applies to the total stewardship of our life.

When we order from a restaurant menu, we choose from its columns. For example, we make our choices from the lunch menu, dinner entrees, desserts, or the daily special column, and for the most part we get what we pay for. We can make menu substitutions, but they may come with an extra cost. Conversely, when we commit ourselves to Christ, we vow to love and obey Him without picking and choosing from His "menu."

The Kingdom of Heaven is an upside-down world. The poor inherit riches. The sorrowing are blessed. And those who follow Jesus gain everything by giving it away. Putting Him first above anyone or anything else. It's not just memorizing His commandments; it's practicing them moment by moment and day by day.

The joy at the center of our Christian experience is reflected in our loving and obedient giving.

RELATED:

"It's one thing to know that God is reliable; it's another thing to actually trust Him. That's the difference between faith and action." – Earle Wilson

MY PRAYER:

Father, as Your child I am duty bound to obey You; but it's from a deep love for who You are and for what You've done for me. Amen.

24

A DEDICATED PLAN

*"On the first day of every week, each one of you should set
aside a sum of money in keeping with your income, saving
it up, so that when I come no collections will have to be made.
Then, when I arrive, I will give letters of introduction to the
men you approve and send them with your gift to Jerusalem"
(1 Corinthians 16:2-3)*

Zero! That's how much 66 million Americans have saved for an emergency expense, according to a survey by Bankrate. Many simply lack the dedication to stick to a budget, which may include putting a designated percentage of their income into a savings account or emergency fund. But when the unexpected happens, they regret their "spend it now" practices.

And then there are frills like upscale vacations, which families enjoy, but are never fun to pay for after the fact (especially when the credit card bill comes.) Both the emergency and the enjoyment times would result in less stress if families dedicated themselves to a plan.

When the New Testament church in Jerusalem faced a financial crisis, the Apostle Paul launched a plan for the Corinthian church that came from the instructions of the Malachi 3:10 tithing plan. The resulting dedicated and organized giving would help their sister church in Jerusalem.

God is a God of order. From the Creation in seven days to the birth of the Christ "in the fullness of times," to the unfolding of the seasons, God does things in order and on schedule.

Right living and right giving fall in line with God's Word that everything has a time and season. And when we determine to surrender our lives totally to Him, we will follow His principles of savings and giving. And notice that it comes "first."

RELATED:

"The principle of First Fruits is a guide for Christians who want to offer themselves and their possessions back to God; "First" gives it the priority that God intended." –David Dean

MY PRAYER:

Lord, give me Your wisdom to live an orderly and productive life for Your glory. Amen.

25

HOARDING

*"But whatever were gains to me I now consider loss for the
sake of Christ. What is more, I consider everything a loss
because of the surpassing worth of knowing Christ Jesus my Lord,
for whose sake I have lost all things" (Philippians 3:7-8a)*

M r. Greenwald lived down a sandy lane in a southern
town. He seemed to live a deprived existence. When
neighbors checked on him, they found opened cans of soup, evidence of his poor eating habits. His house was dark and grim. He
had few friends and no family.

But he had money. Lots of it, tucked away in drawers and
coffee cans or stuffed into furniture cushions. He was a money
hoarder.

Of course, hoarding isn't just about money; and it's prevalent
enough to have its own reality series on cable TV. The series docu-
ments people buying and then saving stuff that's usually stacked
to the ceiling. Hoarders live in the most severe personal conditions to make room for their collections.

Paul was a positive hoarder of sorts. Before his Damascus Road experience (See Acts 9), he collected everything he could to improve his image and his "righteousness" in the eyes of others. But one day Paul met Jesus and found something so valuable he put everything he owned up for auction.

What kind of commitment would cause Paul to give up everything to serve Jesus? The same kind of commitment Jesus expects of us! In Bible times, He told a young leader who asked what he needed to do to have eternal life: "Go, sell everything you have and give to the poor, and you will have treasure in heaven. Then come, follow me" (Mark 10:21b).

A material auction may not be necessary, but the full surrender of our heart is. Giving up everything stored there to make room for Christ and His kingdom.

RELATED:

"One person's gift serves many. That is what God does best: He takes what we give Him and multiplies its effect." – Vera Radley

MY PRAYER:

Jesus, I give You the commitment of my heart. I will keep nothing that stands between us. Amen.

~~~~~~

26

UNWILLING SACRIFICE

*"Who were they who heard and rebelled? Were they not all
those Moses led out of Egypt?" (Hebrews 3:16)*

A riot was brewing. Spies sent from the Israelites reported
possible dangers and hardships Israel might face during
the rest of their journey. A grumbling session was called, and the
complaints could be heard all the way to heaven. "No more! Not
a step farther!" The Israelites who had sacrificed everything to follow Moses out of Egypt rebelled. "We've given enough!"

They were like the people in this story. Erin and Tiffany have
been best friends since Kindergarten. Both lost their fathers at age
13. And both families struggled in the aftermath, financially and
emotionally. Both dreamed of college and marriage and a fulfilling life. Only one achieved it.

Erin took an after school job during high school. She was ac-
cepted to college through the work program and graduated with
honors. She married a hard working, young seminary student,

and together they not only supported their families, they ministered to others.

Tiffany, on the other hand, withdrew, letting her grief color everything in her world. The abuse she had suffered in life made her bitter. She refused to dirty her hands trying to make her future better. She just wouldn't sacrifice anymore.

Rebellion like the Israelites' expresses itself in many ways, according to the people involved. Sometimes it even sits in a modern worship facility, with a scowl on its face. "Another mission project?! Really!" or "Building renovation?! We can't afford one more building program!"

A refusal to sacrifice, to do or give anything more, has deeper implications. A spiritual heart valve is obstructed. After receiving a steady flow of God's blessings, complacency and self-interest have resulted in a blockage. Sometimes we forget that God will never ask more from us than what He already has or will supply.

RELATED:

"All of us have to say 'The Lord has done great things for us.' If He never did another thing, we would still have to say, 'He has done great things for us.'" –Terry Toler

MY PRAYER:

Father, cleanse my heart of any spiritual blockage and use me for Kingdom building. Amen.

~~~~~~

27

ULTIMATE SERVANTHOOD

"Whoever wants to save their life will lose it, but whoever loses their life for me will find it" (Matthew 16:25)

The US Department of State offers a position titled a "Security Protective Specialist." That's bureaucracy-speak for "bodyguard." The list of qualifications is long; the duties are intense and the service location is unknown. And, oh yes, the fine print includes the possibility of death!

Bodyguard is a service career and demands the ultimate servanthood. Those who guard others must be willing to lose their life to save the life of another. A case in point is the Secret Service agent who suffered a mortal wound by taking a bullet intended to assassinate President Ronald Reagan.

Jesus asks us to be servants who would be willing to lose our lives to save someone else. But in this Scripture verse, the life we save is our own: "Whoever loses their life for me will find it." That loss of life may or may not be physical, though for some who have been martyred for their faith, it surely included that. It is our total life; our physical, social, financial, or vocational life. We put it all on the line when we sign up to be on the Jesus team.

Interestingly, Christ Himself seemed to be more comfortable with the title of "servant" than "master." Matthew 20:28, "The Son of Man did not come to be served, but to serve, and to give his life as a ransom for many." And as our "ransom" He displayed "ultimate servanthood," giving His life for ours.

How can we count our losses when we have experienced so many gains? We have no other option than to live as grateful servants. Willing to pay the ultimate price for the One who loved us so much He took our place on the cross that was destined for us.

RELATED:

"Sometimes, we have the resources to fill in the gap for someone who doesn't have sufficient means." –Elmer Towns

MY PRAYER:

Lord, for whatever that may cost me, I declare that I am Your servant. Amen.

2 8

LORD OF ALL

"Take delight in the Lord, and he will give you the desires of your heart" (Psalm 37:4)

Sharon is addicted to soap operas. She has been since she first saw General Hospital as a teen. Now in her 50's, with a family, she feels a little silly living life by proxy, feeling jealous every time one of the silky-haired characters nabs a young intern.

She has kept her secret well; even her husband doesn't know about her daily fix. She knows it's wrong to live in a world of fiction, but it represents all she ever wanted and never got, and probably never will have. She also knows it's wrong to harbor the lustful thoughts that the soaps seem to incite.

Sharon wanted to be a nurse and work in a big hospital with lots of excitement and surrounded by important people. She wanted to know that her life counted for something, like bringing comfort to sick people. Now, all she can hope to taste are the crumbs of others' success. All the joy she has is a few lonely moments in front of a screen, and the guilt that comes with it.

God wants to give us the desires of our hearts, but first our delight must be in Him. He must have our heart. A heart focused on selfish desires does not delight in the Lord; it delights in self. As someone once said, "If Jesus is not Lord of all, He cannot be Lord at all.

We cannot be good stewards of our lives if we refuse to let Him be Lord over every area. Our hearts. Our homes. Our plans. Our relationships. Our finances. That settled, we can expect the joy of His blessing. And we can bless others through joyful service and joyful giving.

RELATED:

"When you respond to God's leadership in joyful giving, it influences everyone around you." - John C. Maxwell

MY PRAYER:

Father, may my desires be in keeping with Your desires for my life. And may the gifts I give to You be filled with the joy You have given me. Amen.

29

THE JOY OF SHARING

"I have seen a grievous evil under the sun: wealth hoarded to the harm of its owners" (Ecclesiastes 5:13)

Katrina was a missionary intern in South America the first time she experienced it. She saw poverty and filth and misery that she could barely have imagined. And when she discovered that supplies shipped to meet those needs were often confiscated by greedy people, her heart was broken.

But what surprised her was the kind generosity of people who suffered by the greed. No matter that they had tiny shacks with cold, dirt floors for homes; scarcity of food to feed their family; and warmth only by sleeping next to their animals. When the missionaries planned to visit them, they would walk for miles to buy fresh vegetables, and then insist on giving the largest portions to their guests.

When the lady of one house gifted the missionary with a small wooden sculpture, Katrina knew it had to be the most precious thing she owned. But this woman who had so little, freely gave it away, knowing the joy of sharing.

When Katrina was reading in Ecclesiastes during her morning quiet time, she came across the Bible verse and thought of the those who deprived others of living essentials, and the evil that must have wreaked havoc in their greedy hearts.

But the problem of hoarding isn't just on a national or regional scale; it can be local, and even personal. Withholding earned or inherited wealth from rightful heirs. Refusing to support a worthy cause because of a personal agenda. Reluctance to give when mission pledges are received in the local church. Withholding goods or services not only impoverishes others, it compromises the spiritual health of the hoarder. It also creates a vacuum of joy that can only be filled by compassionate generosity.

Freely we receive, freely we give. Or, in other words, joyfully we receive, joyfully we share.

RELATED:

"Will you be a part of the giving cycle and generously give to meet the needs of others?"   -George Mueller

MY PRAYER:

Lord, give me an open heart and open hands to reach out to others in need. Amen.

30

NOT-SO-INSTANT REWARDS

"The Lord rewards everyone for their righteousness and faithfulness" (1 Samuel 26:23a)

One charity's website includes a giving calculator. With it, you can figure out the tax savings you will receive from giving to that charity. That way, you can determine the reward you will get for your gift.

Tax deductions are a service of our tax system that not only helps us become good steward-managers of God's resources, they also give us a reward.

Certainly, they are beneficial to those of us who give to charitable organizations, but they are not the primary reason we give. We give out of obedience to God and to express our gratitude for what God has given to us. He exemplified giving in such a loving way by the offering of His Only Son to pay the penalty of our sin.

God not only approves our giving from a righteous heart, He rewards it. "Give and it shall be given to you" (Luke 6:38). But if you're still waiting at the mailbox of earth for a heavenly "return," don't be discouraged. He is the Lord of time and space, including the delivery schedule. In fact, there are dividends that you will never see during your lifetime.

The writer to the Hebrews underscored God's faithfulness: "God is not unjust; he will not forget your work and the love you have shown him as you have helped his people and continue to help them" (Hebrews 6:10). The God who sees in secret keeps flawless records, and the public payoff is not only certain, it is "out of this world!"

In the meantime, He writes checks of mercy morning by morning, gives dividends of grace throughout the day, and often distributes supplies under the shadows of midnight. You can be sure that there will be, in the words of the classic sermon, "Payday Someday."

RELATED:

"God is the endless source of everything. When we give what we have in His name, He keeps the supply coming." – Kevin Myers

MY PRAYER:

Creator God, I give to You from a heart of love and thankfulness. Amen.

A PENNY EARNED

"Dishonest money dwindles away, but whoever gathers little by little makes it grow" (Proverbs 13:11)

In 1902, James Cash Penney opened a store in Kemmerer, Wyoming, with an investment of $2,000. In 1913, after adding 33 more, the stores were incorporated as the J. C. Penney Company. The business grew steadily, and though Penney lost virtually all his personal wealth during the Stock Market Crash of 1929, the corporation recovered and became one of America's major department store chains.

Penney was a Missouri farm boy who learned the value of a dollar from his Baptist preacher father. His father's early death forced James to start clerking in a local store to support the family. Converted to Christianity in a sanatorium, where he was being treated after the great financial crash, Penney became a man who ultimately learned where the greatest value rests: eternal wealth.

Most of us may never have the business success of a J. C. Penney. The convergence of perfect economic landscape, conservative culture, and personal chutzpah that created those Edwardian-age entrepreneurs is rare. But we can apply the principle of gathering and stewarding through honest industry.

Many would be better off financially (including current directors of the store chain) if they were guided by the biblical principles Penney utilized. And frankly, everyone would be better off if they put God in charge of their cash flow. The promised guidance of His Holy Spirit includes spending as well as saving and earning as well as giving. His spiritual checks (inner cautions) give us all a better balance! If nothing else, we would learn the importance of the smallest gains along the road to financial security. Dimes saved become dollars that can be invested and multiplied until they could be the sole funding of a Kingdom ministry.

RELATED:

"If someone wrote your biography, what would it say if all they had to guide them was your checkbook or your income tax return." – David Pitzer

MY PRAYER:

Lord, be the guide of my earnings, my spending, and my savings. And help me to be thankful for the smaller blessings as well as the greater. Amen.

3 2

CONTENTMENT MELTDOWN

"Keep your lives free from the love of money and be content with what you have, because God has said, 'Never will I leave you; never will I forsake you'" (Hebrews 13:5)

Callie stared at her latest online Pinterest board, "Clothes I'd Love to Wear." She was up to 300 "pins" on it already. And it was being followed by quite a few fellow "pinners." Maybe they were like her, wishing for stuff they didn't have. It wasn't that she was dirt poor, but on her husband's retail sales income, their family just didn't have funds for a new wardrobe.

Still, she was tired of wearing the old stuff. The longer she stared at the screen, the more upset she became. And though she knew it was childish to drag out the tired "it's not fair" tag, that's how she felt deep down.

Advertising commercials and social media posts create an environment for contentment meltdowns. It's hard to maintain balance when we're confronted daily with glossy reminders of what we don't have. And while we might need to create boundaries on our screen time, the problem isn't the technology; it's our hearts.

Contentment meltdowns like Callie's are more common in today's culture. The current generation was raised by a previous generation that vowed to give its children what they went without. The over-swing of the pendulum has created a debtor culture that often spends recklessly.

Money isn't evil, the lust for it is. It creates a spiritual infidelity, where one seeks its company at the price of their relationship with God, and the interests of His kingdom. You've probably heard the expression, "If God is all you have left, you have more than enough." That isn't from the lips of someone who has everything they want, but rather from one who has learned to thank God for giving them what they have.

RELATED:

"To be able to bless people with the good things we have, we must be aware of how blessed we are." –Jim Marshall

MY PRAYER:

Father in Heaven, my supreme desire is to love You more than anything this world could ever offer. Amen.

∼∼∼∼∼∼∼∼∼∼∼∼∼∼∼∼∼∼∼∼

3 3

COULD YOU GIVE IT ALL AWAY?

"Jesus answered, 'If you want to be perfect, go, sell your possessions and give to the poor, and you will have treasure in heaven. Then come, follow me'" (Matthew 19:21)

According to the Bureau of Labor Statistics, nearly 600-million people are homeless. A well-known newspaper once asked one of its reporters to masquerade as a homeless person outside the residence of a city official. His mission was to see how long it would take the police to ask him to leave the area. It only took a few minutes.

Being homeless is hardly a bright spot on one's resume. So, it's a bit ironic that in His dealings with the young man we call the Rich Young Ruler, Jesus advised him to sell everything he owned and become a homeless disciple. Yet, Jesus said of Himself, "Foxes have dens and birds have nests, but the Son of Man has no place to lay his head" (Matthew 8:20).

The real issue wasn't about a home or homelessness; it was about valuing one above the other. And obviously, from his response, the Rich Young Ruler chose the home and his possessions.

Christian history is dotted with outstanding servants of God who gave up a life of ease to follow Jesus, and to minister off the grid. Their earthly payoff was in the lives transformed by the message of the gospel.

What is the maximum you could give up to follow Christ? Could you give it all away? He may or may not ask you to do that, but your answer is important. Jesus once asked a disciple, "Do you love me more than these?" (John 21:15b). The disciple was Simon Peter, and the question was about his willingness to surrender his past and his future to serve Christ.

The question is relevant to every follower and servant of Christ.

RELATED:

"Whatever you have to give, God wants to use in a bigger sphere than you could ever dream." –Sandi Patty

MY PRAYER:

Jesus, nothing I have is worth more than knowing and serving You as my personal Savior. Amen.

34

FLYING BOTH FLAGS

"No one can serve two masters. Either you will hate the one and love the other, or you will be devoted to the one and despise the other. You cannot serve both God and money" (Matthew 6:24)

It was brother against brother.

The Civil War raged in America from 1861-1865, the ultimate, awful clash between opposing views and passions. More than slavery divided our nation during those dark days; the conflict had been building for years, fed by vastly different philosophies of government as well as beliefs on personhood. But when war finally broke out, families were forced to choose which flag of allegiance they would fly. And some flew both flags, depending on which army was near.

Jesus said, "No one can serve two masters." This includes political thought and worldview, but the specific example He gave was money. Those who are split between their love of money and their love for God are caught in a war of allegiance. And they can be the casualties of their own "friendly fire."

Mark 3:25, "If a house is divided against itself, that house cannot stand." Put that alongside James 4:1, "What causes fights and quarrels among you? Don't they come from your desires that battle within you?" Here you have the real source of division. A heart flying both flags owes its loyalty to none but itself.

Divided ownership is at the core of the money problem. Anything that hasn't been committed to the Lord is up for grabs. And the enemy of faith will use the opportunity to steal the best from us. Our strategy of resistance is important.

The answer is a unilateral surrender. Laying everything we are and everything we have at the feet of the Master, to follow Him, body, soul, mind, and checkbook.

RELATED:

"We have a God who delights in blessing His people. And He blesses them so that they can, in turn, bless others." –Bret Layton

MY PRAYER:

Father God, only by Your Spirit's power supply can I be a totally devoted follower of Jesus. Amen.

DUNN · MOORE · TOLER

~~~~~~

3 5

THE GRIEF OF GREED

"Some people, eager for money, have wandered from the faith and pierced themselves with many griefs" (1 Timothy 6:10b)

If you're looking for loyalty, you might not look for it in the financial district of Manhattan. There, the greedy drive for success at any and all cost, even to separating from friends working side by side. Affection for money divides, rather than unites.

True loyalty is often found in unlikely environments. For example, go to the places where those who are down on their luck gather in parks and subway terminals, or under highway bridges. There, for the most part, you'll find people loyal to each other. They have no grand titles or posh offices, only makeshift shelters and a common respect for those in their situation.

Of course, poverty has its social challenges. Some living homeless can be just as greedy as those working in the glass-walled towers of finance.

Christ followers are warned to avoid the grief that comes with being entangled in greed. The kind of greed seen in the well-known response of wealthy Industrialist, John D. Rockefeller, when asked how much money is enough: "Just a little bit more."

That's reminiscent of the man in the Bible we know as the Rich Fool. "The ground of a certain rich man yielded an abundant harvest. He thought to himself, 'What shall I do? I have no place to store my crops.' Then he said, 'This is what I'll do. I will tear down my barns and build bigger ones'" (Luke 12:16-18).

He wasn't a fool because he had wealth or vision; he was a fool because wealth and vision HAD HIM. We "wander from the faith" by entangling ourselves in the world's race for a living standard that puts itself first and God's Kingdom second.

RELATED:

"The stewardship of life doesn't begin with you, it begins with God. It is merely acknowledging with every fiber of your faith that he has the ultimate authority over everything." –Dan Schafer

MY PRAYER:

Dear God, help me to be concerned with having more of You and less of the world's stuff. Amen.

~~~~~~~~~~~~~~~~~~~~~~~~~~~~~~~

36

THE GIVING WALL

*"He said to them. . . give back to Caesar what is Caesar's, and
to God what is God's" (Luke 20:25)*

Pastor Martin sat quietly in his office and thought about
the board meeting he had just conducted. The building
committee proposed that for the construction of the church's all-
purpose building, there wouldn't be a "Wall of Givers."

When the worship center was built, a section near its en-
trance included bricks inscribed with the names of donors who
gave $1,000 or more to the project. But funds for the new build-
ing had been raised during the recession, and the committee
wanted to recognize every family that had given sacrificially, no
matter the amount. The irate board member had an issue with the
proposal. As Pastor Martin reflected on the meeting, he wondered
whether her overreaction was because her family's name wouldn't
be engraved on a brick.

Giving is a privileged duty motivated by love and obedience to God. When someone gives for the sake of recognition, it becomes a spiritual issue. Jesus was very clear about it, "Be careful not to practice your righteousness in front of others to be seen by them. If you do, you will have no reward from your Father in heaven" (Matthew 6:1).

We bring tithes and offerings to the Lord's house because they are His. Representatives of His opposition approached Jesus with a trick question. "Is it right to pay taxes to Caesar?" His answer was definitive, "Give back to Caesar what is Caesars, and to God what is God's."

We give to honor Him, not to be listed in a Top Ten. Granted, the acknowledgment of the gift is important, but only as it relates to good recordkeeping. The real issue is obedience to God, and being used as a channel of His blessing.

RELATED:

"The mind of God created and sustains the systems that undergird the economies of the world. He is the source of the elements that are forged into the raw materials that underwrite every currency." – Dennis Kinlaw

MY PRAYER:

Search me, O Lord, and examine my motives for serving in Your name. Amen.

37

CHRIST-FILLED AND CHRIST-LIKE

"Command them to do good, to be rich in good deeds, and to be generous and willing to share. In this way they will lay up treasure for themselves as a firm foundation for the coming age, so that they may take hold of the life that is truly life" (1 Timothy 6:17-19)

Candidates for the nation's highest offices are vetted publicly. And both what they earn and what they give are scrutinized. We could only assume that voters want to know whether candidates making their costly treks to government buildings have compassion as well as industry.

Paul the Apostle would check their giving. He advises the "rich" to be "willing to share." Connect the dots from that advice to the bottom line of the verse, "taking hold of the life that is truly life," and you have an interesting topic for discussion.

"True" life is Christ-filled and Christ-like. The Bible says, "In your relationships with one another, have the same mindset as Christ Jesus" (Philippians 2:5). That leads us back to the proverbial "What would Jesus Do?" question. The Scriptures answer with a portrait of His humility:

- He was rich but became poor, so that we would could become rich.

- He ruled the heavens but was willing to submit to earthly parenting.

- He created the earth but was buried in a borrowed grave.

- He formed the galaxies but noticed the coin a widow contributed.

His whole life was one of humble giving and affirming. Ours should be the same. John wrote, "In this world we are like Jesus" (1 John 4:17b).

We will never be able to duplicate His great sacrifice, but we can die trying.

RELATED:

"When you give Jesus your life as an act of faith in Him, he plants the power of His Greatest Gift into your heart. You have the gift of His wisdom and ability to give every other gift in seed form. Now, you act out of obedience and gratitude for His Great Gift." - Waldo Werning

MY PRAYER:

Lord Jesus, your humble sacrifice for others inspires me to be Your hands and feet in my own world. Amen.

~~~~~~

38

ONE-HUNDRED-PERCENT

*"Calling his disciples to him, Jesus said, 'This poor widow
has put more into the treasury than all the others. They all gave
out of their wealth; but she, out of her poverty, put in everything
— all she had to live on'" (Mark 12:43-44)*

Imagine the pastor's surprise when he looked down from
the platform and noticed a preschooler take a handful of
coins from the offering plate as it passed by. And imagine the
surprise of the child's parents when they spotted the pastor's look,
and then watched the child put the coins into his pockets!

The story is true, but that pastor wasn't the first to eye the
offering plate. Mark records: "Jesus sat down opposite the place
where the offerings were put and watched the crowd putting their
money into the temple treasury. Many rich people threw in large
amounts. But a poor widow came and put in two very small cop-
per coins, worth only a few cents" (Mark 12:41-42).

The nameless widow had no idea that Jesus observed her offering, and had no idea that her small act of worship would be praised through the centuries.

Her offering isn't exemplary because of its amount; its exemplary because of the percentage it represented: One-hundred-percent, "all she had to live on."

But it wasn't just all she had; it was all she was: generous and faithful in her concern for God's kingdom. The beauty of God's expressed standard for giving is that it's the same for every economic group: ten-percent, the tithe. Granted, ten-percent given from wealth will amount to more than ten-percent given from poverty. The important thing is the attitude of the giver. Does it represent "all" of the amount God whispered to their heart? That's the one-hundred-percent He cares about most.

Give all that you have of all that God asks.

RELATED:

"Whole life stewardship is inclusive. It acknowledges from the heart that everything doesn't just come from the Lord, IT IS THE LORD'S." – Ron Schubert

MY PRAYER:

Lord, give me Your grace to be a one-hundred-percent follower of Jesus; spiritually, financially, and in every other way. Amen.

〰〰〰〰〰〰〰〰〰〰

39

PLAN BEFORE YOU BUILD

*"Suppose one of you wants to build a tower. Won't you first
sit down and estimate the cost to see if you have enough
money to complete it" (Luke 14:28)*

By now, most everybody knows Rome wasn't built in a
day. How long did it take? There's a simple answer. It was
founded in 750 B.C., and it's still being built.

Ancient Rome thrived for over 500 years. Probably planned
across many months or years; its straw or wood beginnings
evolved into a beautiful city. Modern Rome continues to be built
from its current plans.

The building project Jesus mentions wasn't of that magnitude. And, it was in the mind rather than on a plot of ground.
His listeners could visualize by local observation towers or even
houses. The lesson wasn't about building materials or construction methods; it was about reminding us to consider the commitment before we act.

Someone once said of failure, "No one plans to fail, they just
fail to plan." The principle is relevant to our spiritual life, as well

as to every other aspect of living. The wisdom writer said, "Commit to the Lord whatever you do, and he will establish your plans" (Proverbs 16:3).

- Plan your devotional times, and He will reveal His truth or presence as needed.

- Plan your service to others, and He will open doors of opportunity to people in need.

- Plan your giving patterns, and He will supply resource and wisdom with which to give.

- Plan your calendar priorities, and He will give direction and power to meet their demands.

Life is too important to play it by ear. It consists of a massive amount of decisions, made every day of every month of every year. And the promise is that if anyone lacks wisdom in its building, they can ask of God and He will give it.

RELATED:

"We make a living through what we get; we make a life through what we give." - Winston Churchill

PRAYER:

Father, I covenant to make Your will my will, so that everything I plan or do is molded, directed, and empowered by You. Amen.

40

WATCH OUT FOR WEEDS

"The seed falling among the thorns refers to someone who hears the word, but the worries of this life and the deceitfulness of wealth choke the word, making it unfruitful" (Matthew 13:22)

When it comes to growing their money, some people have a green thumb. New York City once claimed its Fifth Avenue had two miles of millionaires. Twentieth-century tycoons lived lives of ease, in storied mansions that sprawled along the street. Many used their riches for good, supporting charities and charitable causes. Others used it to feed their own greed, then grudgingly willed it to subsequent generations. Though they grew golden fields of wealth, history records that weeds also grew and choked their lives.

Jesus warned about weed growth during His earthly teachings. In His good-seed/bad-seed, good-soil/bad-soil lesson, He said the seed of God's Word could either bloom and grow or be buried among two species of weeds: The worries of life and the deceitfulness of wealth.

We've passed the industrial age, and are rushing through the digital age, but the threat is as real now as it was then.

The "deceitfulness of wealth" is a strange concept to our culture. We hear more about wealth's advantages. Infomercials and best-sellers preach its value. Celebrities give TV tours through their luxury homes, pointing out the pricey and priceless along the way. And promises of lottery winnings incite the impoverished to gamble away their grocery money.

Deceitfulness suggests hiding truth. The truth is, wealth has a dark side. Promising freedom, it often brings bondage. Worries about its gains and losses can grow like weeds and choke the spirit of its worriers. Spiritually, weeds of selfishness can grow quietly in our garden of godliness.

Mark 8:36, "What good is it for someone to gain the whole world, yet forfeit their soul?"

RELATED:

"God has promised to supply our daily necessities. Beyond that, we must answer the question of what we will do with the excess." – Craig Dunn

MY PRAYER:

Spirit of God, help me to be open to Your guidance about my spiritual and financial health. And may my heart be free of weeds. Amen.

~~~~~~~~~~~~~~~~~~~~~~~~~~~~~~~~~~~~

41

PAY IT FORWARD

"From time to time those who owned land or houses
sold them, brought the money from the sales and put
it at the apostles' feet, and it was distributed to anyone
who had need" (Acts 4:34-35)

Bud and Sandy wrapped their arms around their friends. Together, they stood before the smoking embers that once was their friends' home. Bud spoke first, "Larry, we are so sorry for your loss. As your brothers and sisters in Christ, we prayed before we got out of the car, and decided that we are going to put our house on the market, and donate the money to you through our church."

That may seem almost absurd today. But in first century church times, that kind of pay-it-forward transaction was not uncommon. The Bible says of those Christians, "No one claimed that any of their possessions was their own" (Acts 4:32b).

According to a census.gov news release, during last year's Thanksgiving holidays, nearly 600-thousand new homes were sold nationwide, at an average price of over $300-thousand dollars. And we could guess that very, very few of those homes were donated to someone who had lost theirs.

In church history's toughest times, its members made their greatest sacrifices. First-century Christians were shunned and denied the basics of life. Now, in many countries, that church history is repeating itself in a tragic way. Paying it forward has literally meant paying with someone's own life.

One thing different about today's church is its cultures and customs. God's supply from the riches of heaven is the same. Eternal life through faith in Jesus Christ is the same. The fellowship of believers is the same. The biblical standard for giving is the same. Could it be that our thinking about the needs of others has changed? Are we more in a keeping mode than a pay-it-forward mode?

RELATED:

"Even when we have earned what we have, it was really God who enabled us to do that." – Larry Moore

MY PRAYER:

Lord, change the customs of my heart and help me to be in a pay it forward mode. Amen.

<hr>

4 2

A LEGACY OF FIRST FRUITS

"Honor the Lord with your wealth, with the firstfruits of all your crops; then your barns will be filled to overflowing, and your vats will brim over with new wine" (Proverbs 3:9-10)

Jason stood on his back porch and looked over the land that stretched out as far as he could see. It was his now; a farm that had been in his family for generations was entrusted to his hands. At only forty-years-old, he was a bit awed at the responsibility, yet eager to get out and plunge his hands into his very own soil.

The story of how his great, great-grandfather had settled this homestead at great cost had been passed down. He had fought wildfires, disease, and drought to birth the first crop. And then, in an act of faith, he donated a large percentage of the proceeds from that crop to build a little white church. The first in that farming community.

Grandfather Jacobsen believed in honoring God with the first and best of his increase, as a part of good financial stewardship. And Jason's family was still being blessed because of it.

Jason thought about it during the dedication ceremony for a new community center his church had just built. The little white church was gone now, replaced with a sprawling campus that housed ministries for hundreds of families in a growing community. He thanked God for the opportunity to continue the legacy of giving a percentage of the farm's income to the Lord.

Jason and his wife, Vicki, were raising their family in a culture totally unlike that of their parents and grandparents. Blessed financially, they struggled to teach their children spiritual and financial values. Giving their "firstfruits" in obedience to God's Word was not just personally and spiritually beneficial, it directly influenced their children.

RELATED:
"We manage all that God has given to us on His behalf, and use it for His purposes." – Doug Carter

MY PRAYER:
Lord of the Harvest, I bow before You in thanksgiving for Your blessings and pledge to use them for Your honor. Amen.

~~~~~~

43

PRINCE AND PAUPER ALIKE

*"The cries of the harvesters have reached the ears of the
Lord Almighty" (James 5:4b)*

Mark Twain's classic, The Prince and the Pauper, was set
in 1547. He wrote of its economic conditions, "Broken heads were as common as hunger in that place. Yet little Tom
was not unhappy. He had a hard time of it, but did not know it."

Tom Canty, a character in the novel, didn't know he was subjected to a life of poverty. Conversely, the character, Prince Edward, knew nothing but luxury.

Class warfare between the haves and have-nots has been going on for ages. The cry for fairness has been a long one, but God's
love cares for the prince and pauper alike. God values no person above another. Acts 17:26 (NKJV), "He has made from one
blood every nation of men to dwell on all the face of the earth."

The ground is level before His throne. And none move an
inch closer because of the size of their portfolio. God expects the

same of His kingdom citizens. There is no select seating; it's all general admission. James 2:3-4, "If you show special attention to the man wearing fine clothes and say, 'Here's a good seat for you,' but say to the poor man, 'You stand there' or 'Sit on the floor by my feet,' have you not discriminated among yourselves." He commands us to deal impartially with everyone and to be honest in our dealings.

We all get into the kingdom through the same Door (John 10:7). We all benefit from the same grace. And we all utilize our talents for the same heavenly purpose. Likewise, we all contribute to the same mission: World evangelism and discipleship.

The mission is fair. Everyone participates as they are resourced by God's supply and enabled by God's Spirit.

RELATED:

"The church is commissioned to go into all the world and preach the gospel. It's a "great commission" that demands great support." – T.M. Anderson

MY PRAYER:

Lord Jesus, thank You for giving me an opportunity to be a part of the greatest mission in all the world. Amen.

〰〰〰〰〰〰〰〰〰〰

44

WILLING RESPONSE

*"The people rejoiced at the willing response of their leaders,
for they had given freely and wholeheartedly to the Lord. David
the king also rejoiced greatly" (1 Chronicles 29:9)*

Many moms sacrifice for their young but none do it quite as wholeheartedly as the black lace weaver spider. A few days after she hatches her young, she encourages them to make her body their lunch. That's giving your all!

God calls us to willingness in our giving, sometimes even when it's painful. He is, after all, the Provider and Sustainer. As we obey His Word, the obligation is on Him to care for us.

Throughout Scripture, we can find examples of willing responses of money and other resources. When Israel contributed to the building of the Temple, everyone gave their best and rejoiced that those who led them in the offering were first to give. King David, father of the general contractor, King Solomon, said of his gift, "In my devotion to the temple of my God, I now give my personal treasures of gold and silver."

Christians in the New Testament had such a willingness to give that they "gave as much as they were able, and even beyond their ability. Entirely on their own" (2 Corinthians 8:3).

Willingness is the crucible of devotion to God. At that altar, we confess what we bring to our relationship with Him. Abraham modeled that in his willingness to offer his own son, Isaac, on the altar of sacrifice. During the climb, Isaac asked a heartbreaking question, "Where is the lamb for the sacrifice." In unwavering faith, Abraham replied, "The Lord will provide."

As someone once said, "Give 'til it helps." And the one it helps most are those who have given themselves along with their gifts, as Jesus did at the Cross. Right living is the precursor for right giving.

RELATED:

"Faith in human resources brings minimal results. Faith in God's resources brings mountainous results." –O.D. Emery

MY PRAYER:

Father God, I give to You from my complete devotion to You. Accept my willingness as a sacrifice of worship. Amen.

4 5

THE NAME ON EVERY ACCOUNT

"The world is mine, and all that is in it" (Psalm 50:12)

"List your assets." Kayla looked at the line on the paperwork she and her husband were filling out and sighed. They didn't own much. Their little starter house still belonged to the bank and they didn't even own the titles to their well-worn vehicles. They were doing their best to be good stewards and were occasionally making double payments. But starting out as a young married couple didn't equal being financially set.

Most of us start life without the proverbial silver spoon in our mouth. In fact, many of us had to settle for plastic. Born to wealth isn't a description the average person claims.

Our Heavenly Father, on the other hand, owns, well . . . everything. There is no continent that is not part of His domain, no bank account that does not bear His unseen signature.

For us, "Owner" is a nametag proudly worn. It may represent work beyond the call of duty or stress to the edge physical or emotional collapse. So, when that product or property is in hand, we claim ownership. But do we really?

The signature of the Sovereign Lord seals any deal a Christ-follower transacts. His name is on every account. Every ounce of strength, every act of wisdom, and every creative thought comes from Him, and belongs to Him. We are debtors without the greatest debt: the guilt of our past. We are filled with both a holy presence and a holy inheritance. All of heaven is ours because we decided to quit living for the earth, even while we travel it.

The fact is, through faith in Christ, we have been born again with the "silver spoon" of salvation in our heart, purchased with the priceless blood of Jesus. Our riches are not in what we own, but rather in what we have signed-off to follow Him.

RELATED:

"Everything we do for God and the good of others will happen in the swift interlude we know as time." – J.D. Abbott

MY PRAYER:

Father, You are both the Giver and the Owner; I am the grateful manager. Amen.

46

HONOR THE SOURCE

"But remember the Lord your God, for it is he who gives you the ability to produce wealth, and so confirms his covenant, which he swore to your ancestors, as it is today" (Deuteronomy 8:18)

Any people or nation that doesn't believe it was created by, and dependent upon God is foolish. At least that's what the Word of God says, "The fool says in his heart, 'There is no God.' They are corrupt, and their ways are vile; there is no one who does good" (Psalm 53:1b). That may not have a politically correct ring to it, but its absolute truth has been on top shelf display from the beginning.

First generation people made a dangerous stop on their biblical journey. Israel stopped depending on God and started depending on self. Turning their eyes from God's provision, they formed a building committee, "Come, let us build ourselves a city, with a tower that reaches to the heavens, so that we may make a name for ourselves" (Genesis 11:4b). In the vernacular, we might ask, "And how is that working out for you?" It didn't. Their purpose was a show of force, but the result was a loss of power, mass confusion, and cultural division.

The physical or financial resources of any people are on loan from one true source: "Remember the Lord your God, for it is he who gives you the ability to produce wealth."

Right living comes from a right relationship with that Source: "If you remain in me and I in you, you will bear much fruit; apart from me you can do nothing" (John 15:5b). He is the source of purity for the soul, provision for living, and power for service.

Be careful of building do-it-yourself towers. You could put your soul in harm's way, take a fall, and break your spirit.

RELATED:

"God's approval is worth infinitely more than human applause. If it's a choice between great buildings and God's blessing, choose God's blessing." – Jim Dunn

MY PRAYER:

Father God, remind me when I begin to build towers of self rather than seeking more of You as my truest source. Amen.

~~~~~~

47

ABUNDANT RESPONSIBILITY

"Yours, Lord, is the greatness and the power and the glory and the majesty and the splendor, for everything in heaven and earth is yours. Yours, Lord, is the kingdom; you are exalted as head over all. Wealth and honor come from you" (1 Chronicles 29:11-12)

He never understood the term "American arrogance" until his first tour of duty in Afghanistan. Its citizens' ragged clothing, crowded hovels, and food scarcity had given him a much deeper understanding of why Americans were viewed in that way.

Private Jeffery Gordon would never look at his own abundance in quite the same way. Sure, he came from a middle-class family; they weren't rich, but compared to the conditions he saw overseas, they had an abundance.

Reflecting on his tour of duty, Jeff was glad for the Christian worldview he was taught in his formative years. He knew that God alone allows wealth and prosperity; and that abundant blessings come with responsibility. As Jesus said, "From everyone who has been given much, much will be demanded" (Luke 12:48b).

Now that he had a family of his own, Jeff, along with his wife, needed to apply that in real time teachings. They focused on five:

- First, they would teach their children that possessions were gifts from God and that His gifts should be paid forward.

- Second, they would teach wisdom in making purchases; involving their children in discussions about true needs and comparison shopping.

- Third, they would teach their children to tithe as soon as they were old enough to understand.

- Fourth, they would make lifestyle choices based on the principles of God's Word and the leading of the Holy Spirit.

- Fifth, they would learn about the stewardship of life as a family; using their time, talent, and tithes in church ministries.

Jeff's family grew through the practice, until they could pray with the psalmist, "You brought us to a place of great abundance" (Psalm 66:12, NLT).

RELATED:

"Every time you offer your abilities in Christ's service, you give from the abundance you received, and someone will be blessed." –Terry Munday

MY PRAYER:

Lord, make me a teacher of your abundant blessings, Amen.

∿∿∿∿∿∿∿∿∿∿∿∿∿∿∿∿∿∿∿∿∿

48

RIGHT PREPARATION

"One person gives freely, yet gains even more; another withholds unduly, but comes to poverty. A generous person will prosper; whoever refreshes others will be refreshed" (Proverbs 11:24-25)

When the Titanic first sailed in April 1912, she carried a wide spectrum of passengers. They included emigrants in the third-class section, working class tourists in second class, and aristocrats and socialites in first class.

Within five days, the unthinkable happened. The Titanic struck an iceberg and sank. Lifeboats were lowered, but in the confusion, many were only partially filled. And in a sad testament to the class system of the time, a greater percentage of those in third class were lost than any other passenger group.

Survivors said some saved themselves by sneaking into lifeboats meant only for women and children, only to die in bankruptcy later. They also said some sacrificed their lives so others could be saved, and gained fame and posthumous wealth later.

Right living and right giving include right preparation. The first, and most important, is preparing the soul for eternal life. Jesus cautioned, "Be dressed ready for service and keep your lamps burning, like servants waiting for their master to return from a wedding banquet, so that when he comes and knocks they can immediately open the door for him" (Luke 12:35-36). Every Christ follower has a spiritual checklist in their mind, with marks or empty spaces that gauge their readiness for either sudden death or Christ's sudden return.

Another preparation is financial. Since we don't know when Christ will return, we need a financial plan that reflects good stewardship beyond our life and death on earth. Many can provide more resources for fulfilling Christ's mission after their death than they could during their lifetime. Right giving doesn't stop at the grave; it goes beyond, designating funds for ministry through estate plans.

But with the Apostle Paul, we can testify, "whether we live or die, we belong to the Lord."

RELATED:

"An estate plan is the last stop on your roadmap to personal financial stewardship." – Larry Moore

MY PRAYER:

Lord Jesus, give me wisdom to be a good manager of Your resources in life or in death. Amen.

49

THE RIGHT INGREDIENTS

"Woe to you, teachers of the law and Pharisees, you hypocrites! You give a tenth of your spices—mint, dill and cumin. But you have neglected the more important matters of the law—justice, mercy and faithfulness. You should have practiced the latter, without neglecting the former" (Matthew 23:23)

Garlic is #1. A national survey determined that for most households, garlic is the spice used most. Its flavor is hidden in many foods, from fried chicken to tortilla chips. If used right, we taste just a hint that comes from the right dash of the spice in the recipe.

The right "ingredients" for victorious Christian living don't include a "dash" of anything. It's full ingredients ahead! Jesus said if we're not with Him, we're against Him. A classic gospel song said, "All for Jesus! All for Jesus! All my being's ransomed powers; all my thoughts and words and doings, all my days and all my hours."

Following Christ isn't choosing between a "standard version" and an "upgrade," like a software app. We chose the "upgrade" at the beginning. Jesus said, "I have come that they may have life, and have it to the full" (John 10:10b). We chose a life full of rights and privileges, but also a life of responsibilities and duties.

Right living includes right giving. And the giving standard is the tithe, giving a tenth of our income back to the Lord (who gave it to us to begin with). Religious revisionists have tried to bend the rule, but like every rule of God, it is as important today as it was when its principle was first delivered (See Malachi 3:10). It's teachable. It's orderly. It's fair. It's productive.

Tithing isn't "in place of." Jesus commended those who tithed, but reminded them not to forget the rest. We, too, need to make sure that we are using the right ingredients, adding offerings to our tithes, adding mercy and justice to our witness, and adding obedience to our faithfulness.

RELATED:

"God blesses generosity. Resources flow to those who use them well." – Dorothy Whipp

MY PRAYER:

Father God, may I never be content to give You the minimum of anything. Amen.

50

GOD'S MEASURING CUP

"Give, and it will be given to you. A good measure, pressed down, shaken together and running over, will be poured into your lap. For with the measure you use, it will be measured to you" (Luke 6:38)

Last year, the manufacturers of Pyrex® bakeware introduced a measuring cup that made it to Guinness World Records. Standing 4-feet tall, the glass receptacle holds over 3-thousand cups of materials, and was filled with popcorn for its debut. On the company's pyrex.com website, their brand manager said of the record-breaker, "This is just the start!"

Both the measuring cup and the manager's vision are bigger than life. But the promise Jesus made about the returns on our giving is even bigger, "Give and it will be given to you." We really can't measure that promise, but neither can we measure any other promise He has made.

We only know that it will exceed our normal expectations. We'll need a cup big enough to hold "pressed down, shaken together, and running over" blessings. Blessings that are "new each morning," God's Word says.

When we do business with God, we should always expect His overpayment. King David said of his interactions with the Almighty, "Surely you have granted him unending blessings and made him glad with the joy of your presence" (Psalm 21:6). God's gifts always have an added value.

So, why does our heart sometimes weaken when we plan our giving during recessionary times? Or, why do clouds of worry creep in when we hold an electric bill in our hand and glimpse the missions pledge envelope on our desk?

In the vernacular, we might say that God is generous to a fault. We can't out give Him. So when we listen to our brothers and sisters in Christ who've given it a try and testify of God's returns, we say inside, "My turn!"

RELATED:

"The first step to financial freedom may seem counterproductive, but it is biblically and practically sound. You start by giving your money away." – Stanley Tam

MY PRAYER:

Father in Heaven, you have always kept your Word to me. Amen.

5 1

BLESSED AND BLESSING

*"In everything I did, I showed you that by this kind of
hard work we must help the weak, remembering the words
the Lord Jesus himself said: 'It is more blessed to give
than to receive'" (Acts 20:35)*

Dylan has Down's syndrome, but he doesn't know it. He's a happy little boy of six, with a big smile and love for teddy bears. But at times he has a stubborn streak that causes him to depend on others to do things he could do himself.

Enter Mrs. Caldwell, a skilled and patient teacher who has given her life to teaching boys and girls like Dylan. She sees beyond their perceived weakness, and teaches them how to use their real strengths to learn and thrive.

Staff who work with her say she models Jesus' words that giving is more blessed than getting. Tired at the end of the day, she is strengthened in the rich knowledge that she has spent another day fulfilling her calling.

The moment someone finds "their place in life" is exciting. And when they discover their "place" is a place of giving it is life-transforming. The greatest evidence of spiritual maturity is found in someone's determination to bless, rather than be blessed.

Isaiah's prophecy of the Messiah Jesus is a great lesson. "The Spirit of the Sovereign Lord is on me, because the Lord has anointed me to proclaim good news to the poor. He has sent me to bind up the brokenhearted, to proclaim freedom for the captives and release from darkness for the prisoner" (Isaiah 61:1). Jesus spent His earthly journey using that blessing to bless others.

If you've ever wondered about "your place," study the prophecy of the Messiah, and then follow Him through the Gospels. Watch how Jesus proved that blessing others is a blessing in itself.

RELATED:

"As God blesses us, we grow to realize that all His blessings are not for us, and allow His goodness to flow through us." – Kent Hubbard

MY PRAYER:

Lord, your blessings to me could never be contained. Help me to share their overflow with others. Amen.

5 2

LAUREN'S CHOICE

"If anyone has material possessions and sees a brother or sister in need but has no pity on them, how can the love of God be in that person?" (1 John 3:17)

Lauren averted her eyes from the person holding a poster at the intersection. It was frequented by people holding similar signs: "No work. Hungry. Anything appreciated. God bless."

She had to make a choice. She heard stories of Good Samaritans being "burned." And too, as a young woman, she felt uneasy about rolling down her window in a neighborhood known for its high crime rate. So, not knowing what she should or could do, she refused to make eye contact, inwardly urging the stoplight to change. Green made the choice for her.

John said we should pity the needy out of our love for God. But does pity have a perimeter? And who draws the lines?

Before Pentecost, Christ's disciples didn't understand the "advantage" Jesus promised in that upper room meeting. He told them it was better for Him to go away; that He was sending the Holy Spirit to take His place. His presence would be everywhere, anytime.

Now, those times they wished Jesus was present to offer advice, when He was teaching or preaching in another region, were over. The Comforter had come, the Holy Spirit would indwell, empower, and enlighten believers. He would bring the wisdom of heaven to every choice.

Right living is Spirit-led living. It looks for directions in the Bible, or listens to His "starts" or "stops" in the heart. Lauren was a believer, but the music on the car radio was so loud it distracted her from listening for the Spirit's voice.

We don't know what He would have said to Lauren about contributing to the sign-holders. We just know from experience when His voice is guiding our own choices.

RELATED:

"If any of you lacks wisdom, you should ask God, who gives generously to all without finding fault, and it will be given to you" (James 1:5).

MY PRAYER:

Spirit of God, help me to be a careful listener for the leadings of Your Spirit. Amen.

53

TRUST AND TRUSTEES

"I have learned to be content whatever the circumstances"
(Philippians 4:11)

Getting older isn't for the weak, but it usually comes with the territory. And "learning to be content" in that strange new environment takes some of the bravado we lost on the journey.

Often, the sun seems to set too quickly for us, leaving fast-growing shadows of unfamiliar emotional, spiritual, physical, and financial challenges.

Maturity can also bring financial loss, and in some cases, poverty. Metlife Mature Market Institute estimates older Americans suffer the loss of $2.9-billion annually to financial abuse. And in 34-percent of those cases, family members or acquaintances are the perpetrators.

Tactical adjustments are needed. The first is spiritual. Discontent with things around us may be symptomatic of discontent within us. The intensity of our devotional life and Christian service may fade, leaving us more susceptible to discouragement. The remedy is found in a spiritual revival of prayer and Bible study, plus finding a place of service.

The second is physical. It's easier to trade the best for the most convenient. Dietary choices are lost in the crowd of so many other options; it may be easier to skip them. But healthy food trade-offs can be accompanied by re-purposed exercise routines. Now, when someone tells you to "take a walk," they may have your well-being in mind!

The third tactical adjustment is financial. Discontent may accompany incomplete planning. Researching online information with guidance from a certified financial planner can help you establish wills and trusts that will be good for your estate. They will also be good for you, bringing you peace of mind. It's never too late in the journey to plan the last steps.

Most of all, put your trust in the Ultimate Trustee: God. Proverbs 3:6, NLT, "Seek his will in all you do, and he will show you which path to take."

RELATED:

"The purpose of estate planning is to eliminate uncertainty and maximize the value of the estate by reducing taxes and other expenses." – Art Evans

---

MY PRAYER:

Lord, give me wisdom to be a good steward of Your blessings through my financial legacy. Amen.

D U N N · M O O R E · T O L E R

5 4

WHAT GOD ASKS

*"Give generously to them and do so without a
grudging heart; then because of this the Lord your
God will bless you in all your work and in everything you
put your hand to" (Deuteronomy 15:10)*

There was nothing she could do. Moloch required it. It was the price of his favor. The totally horrendous act of child sacrifice to the heathen god had reached her own home. Her husband took the infant from her arms and handed him to the priest.

The bronze statue in the Valley of Hinnom, with a hollow space heated by fire, was the place where the ancient tribes of Canaan made their evil offerings. God warned His people about this abomination. And soon He would bring a deadly judgment upon them.

Compare the horror of that offering with another offering setting. There, Jesus smiled with love and approval as a widow put her last coins into the Temple offering receptacle. Her sacrifice can't be compared to the agony of that family in Canaan, but still, it was all she had. It wasn't without cost, but it wasn't given in fear.

God, our Heavenly Father, asks us to give generously, not to earn His favor or avert His wrath, but to help us grow in faith, and to introduce others to His holiness and forgiveness. He asks us to sacrifice, a reasonable portion of our abundance. Then, from His heart of love, He gives back.

At the heart of our worship is obedience out of love. A full, spiritual exchange of our self-righteousness for God's holy righteousness, given the moment we accept Christ as Savior. And what happens next, harsh reproof for our past? No, quiet and complete forgiveness, and favor on all we do in His name from that time forward.

RELATED:

"Whether or not we receive remarkable compensation for our generosity, we can be grateful knowing that we have been delivered from the futility of chasing things and given the privilege of meeting the needs of others." –Nina Gunter

MY PRAYER:

Dear God, thank You for giving me the opportunity to experience Your love through my obedience to You. Amen.

55

WHEN I GROW UP

"Whoever pursues righteousness and love finds life, prosperity and honor" (Proverbs 21:21)

How many times were you asked, "What do you want to be when you grow up?" Like others, your answers were across the board. They probably included firefighter, police officer, nurse, doctor, singer, actor, teacher, pastor, president, and so forth. One little boy said when he grew up he wanted to be tall!

Sometimes the answers were linked to the payoff. Especially in a day when the rich and famous sport trophies of their success, and their stories spread through the media like marbles dropped on tile flooring.

For the believer, there is only one answer that has an immediate and future significance, and crosses all generational lines: "When I grow up I want to be like Jesus." Pursuing a career or setting a goal won't insure fame or fortune, or even peace of mind. And pursuing excellence without righteousness is a frail objective.

Since we're in varied stages of personal and spiritual growth, the Scriptures give us direction: Peter wrote, "grow in the grace and knowledge of our Lord and Savior Jesus Christ" (2 Peter 3:18); and Paul wrote, "speaking the truth in love, we will grow to become in every respect the mature body of him who is the head, that is, Christ" (Ephesians 4:15).

God promises us prosperity, but it doesn't come with a blank check. It is more of a paycheck. No, we aren't righteous because we earned it; we're righteous because we pursued it. And the payoff was "life, prosperity, and honor." Seeking and finding Christ through faith, we are made righteous to live and love and serve Him.

RELATED:

"By coming to our world as a babe in a manger, Christ stripped Himself of His royal garments and shared them with us. His gift cost His very life's blood. But through His grace, we can be clothed in His righteousness." – O.W. Willis

MY PRAYER:

Lord Jesus, in gratitude for Your gift of righteousness, I covenant to grow in my faith and in my witness to others. Amen.

POWER OF THE CHECKBOOK

"Do not withhold good from those to whom it is due, when it is in your power to act" (Proverbs 3:27)

Tanner is a barista, spending his day behind a counter in a coffee shop with pendant lights and butcher block tables. He serves foamy lattes and dark espressos to teens and collegians and soccer moms and office workers.

Hugo works on a coffee estate in Brazil. He spends eight to ten hours of his day in the sun or rain, harvesting the beans that make America's favorite morning brew.

Paul is a missionary in Brazil. He has seen the abuse of the plantation owners toward their workers. And he knows the western desire to import cheap coffee and make a profit in trendy shops. Paul has a twofold mission: to share the Gospel of Christ and to be a negotiator, working to bring the fair-trade agreement to the plantation where Hugo works.

Few of us can do anything in person about the working conditions of those who produce goods. But most all of us have the power of the checkbook. Guided by the Holy Spirit, our checkbook can be a tool that brings justice and holiness to our culture. Deuteronomy 15:7, "If anyone is poor among your fellow Israelites in any of the towns of the land the Lord your God is giving you, do not be hardhearted or tightfisted toward them."

Giving is a good habit, but it can become routine. Write a check, put it in the envelope, and mail. Go online, put in a password and credit card number, and click. But we can avoid the routine by taking a moment to pray about the distribution of the gift, and the mission of the receiving individual or organization. Now, that's powerful!

RELATED:

"Heaven hasn't downsized. God's resources aren't subject to budget cuts. So, when you're on the expecting side of an investment, you can look for a lavish return." – Rick Harvey

MY PRAYER:

Lord, thank You that I can be a channel of Your blessing. Guide me to the need, and give me an obedient heart. Amen.

57

AMBIDEXTROUS GIVING

"But when you give to the needy, do not let your left hand know what your right hand is doing, so that your giving may be in secret. Then your Father, who sees what is done in secret, will reward you"
(Matthew 6:3-4)

If you can write with either the left or right hand, you are part of an elite one-percent of the population. Handedness is decided in the brain, with right-handers having left-hemisphere dominant brains and most lefties having symmetrical hemispheres.

We don't know which hand Jesus wrote with, but in this portion of the Sermon on the Mount, He was referring not to physical handedness, but to a giving ambidexterity that operates in quiet generosity.

At first, the left hand-right hand reference is a bit confusing. Obviously, both are connected to the same processing center, which sends action commands to our extremities. But Jesus' instruction isn't a matter of outward, physical actions, but rather of inward, spiritual actions. It's like our giving saying to our brain, "Privacy please!"

If it were outward, we might brag about it, and reward ourselves for our generosity. But since it's a spiritual sacrifice, we give without thought of reward. We are ambidextrous givers, giving from the right or left, but giving from the same source and strength: God's resources.

We don't give to get praise; we give for purpose. It's the same in living; we don't live to get praise, we live for purpose. And the purpose is to love, honor, and obey Jesus Christ. That driving force takes the drudgery and duty out, and fills us with joy! Psalm 28:7, The Lord is my strength and my shield; my heart trusts in him, and he helps me. My heart leaps for joy, and with my song I praise him."

RELATED:

"God has chosen to give us the freedom to choose or reject His work in us. Our spiritual life depends on our response to what He offers, our surrender to His plan." – Richard Grindstaff

MY PRAYER:

Father, search my motive for giving to others. And receive all the glory. Amen.

58

LAYER ON LAYER

"From his abundance we have all received one gracious blessing after another" (John 1:16, NLT)

"Daddy, who owns all this stuff in your truck?" Darin looked down at his five-year-old daughter and smiled. Though not yet in Kindergarten, she had the curiosity of a university researcher, and the vocabulary to match.

"Here, baby girl, let me lift you up, and let's talk about it." Darin swung little Lyndsey up to his lap in the driver's seat and placed her tiny hands on the huge steering wheel. "Who owns all this stuff?" He continued, "Well, it belongs to stores. I deliver it to them, and they sell it to people who come to shop."

"And then they'll have more stuff?"

"I guess so, honey. More than they need, maybe."

"Do we have more than we need?"

Darin nodded, "Probably, sweetheart, probably."

Thinking about his blessings, piled one layer on top of another, he was grateful for the lessons in stewardship he had learned as a youngster. He was taught that abundance is a stepping stone to greater blessing, if surrendered to God and used wisely.

Abundance is a word that God can use to bless us, and a word the devil can use to abuse us. Guilt is one of the enemy's primary weapons. "Look at all this stuff you have. Millions of people in this world have nothing, and you bless God for all this!" His subtle accusations are like fiery darts that stick in your armor of faith.

But the devil only knows loss. "The thief comes only to steal and kill and destroy" (John 10:10a), while God only knows giving. "I have come that they may have life, and have it to the full" (John 10:10b). The devil hates your blessings. That's why, at times, you feel miserable about them. Abandon the misery, and praise the Lord for His layered blessings!

RELATED:

"The surrendered life is a blessed life. It is the victorious life. It is the life that experiences God's good purposes." –R.G. Flexon

MY PRAYER:

Lord Jesus, defeat the enemy's purpose to steal the joy of Your blessing on my life. Amen.

5 9

BEYOND THE VALEDICTORIAN'S ADDRESS

*"Since you excel in everything--in faith, in speech, in knowledge, in
complete earnestness and in the love we have kindled in you--see
that you also excel in this grace of giving" (2 Corinthians 8:7)*

Not every high school valedictorian rises to the level of
their speech. For some, it was their only moment in the
spotlight.

The Chicago Tribune reported a study of valedictorians, a
decade after their graduation. Though the honored students had
professional careers, and some with measurable success, they
weren't the movers and shakers of their generation.

More often they moved with the status quo, rather than leading the pack. Certainly, the world needs all sorts of individuals
and temperaments to keep things going. A kitchen with more
chefs than cooks would be a "tossed salad." But a kitchen full
of cooks needs a chef who will rise above the confusion and
give direction.

The Apostle Paul commended first-century Christians in Corinth for the way they excelled in so many things. For the most part, they "played by the rules," but he wanted them to excel in one area: their giving.

Why is giving such an important barometer of spiritual growth? Because if one treasures what they have more than they treasure their relationship with Christ, they will soon seek more of treasures than more of Christ. A New Testament figure, Demas, was a living illustration. He was an associate of Paul who became distracted to the point of abandoning ministry. Paul said of him, "Demas has deserted me because he loves the things of this life" (2 Timothy 4:10, NLT). He was a "spiritual valedictorian" who settled for the status quo.

Heaven doesn't have an accountant that sorts through giving records. It has a Savior who calls and then strengthens the faithful to live above the norm, and give beyond the expected.

RELATED:

"Which of your possessions are enabling you to serve God more fully, and which have become distractions or, worse, deterrents to doing God's will?" –Curt Lewis

MY PRAYER:

Lord, search my heart for any desire to live a status quo life instead of an excellent one. Amen.

~~~~~~~~~~~~~~~~~~~~~~~~~~~~~~~

60

THE WORST INVADER

*"Then he said to them, 'Watch out! Be on your guard
against all kinds of greed; life does not consist in an
abundance of possessions'" (Luke 12:15)*

Kevin owns a home security business, installing the latest
security technology in the plush estates of Panama City,
Florida. Almost daily he works in an environment of luxurious
properties. And business is booming. Owners are willing to spend
high dollars to protect their investments. For many of them, it's
not just about the possessions; it's about the self-esteem associated
with them.

Kevin is also a pastor. He delivers his heart in three messages
each week to a small, inner city church. Nothing is posh there.
Meetings are in a storefront, with folding chairs and a borrowed
keyboard. Many of his congregants are homeless. Yet, Kevin says
there is more spiritual wealth in that place than in most of the
mansions he sees through the week.

He has often thought that what the wealthy really need is a security system that protects against greed. Of all the invaders that can steal from his customers, greed may be the worst. It inflates self-opinion but robs of self-respect.

Not all wealth is associated with greed. There are countless men and women who have gained wealth and yet maintained Kingdom-first values. To them, the greatest wealth is in their relationship with God, and their abundance is counted in blessings as well as dollars. But they too are vulnerable, "No temptation has overtaken you except what is common to mankind" (1 Corinthians 10:13a). So, their strategy is taken from the same verse, "God is faithful; he will not let you be tempted beyond what you can bear. But when you are tempted, he will also provide a way out so that you can endure it" (V. 10:13b). So, they look for the way out.

RELATED:

"Having money is not a sin. On the contrary, the Bible urges us to be diligent and industrious so that we can provide for others and ourselves." – Daniel LeRoy

MY PRAYER:

Father, thank You for warning me about greed, and thank You for power to overcome it. Amen.

~~~~~~~~~~~~~~~~~~~~~~~~~~~

6 1

GODLINESS INDEX

*"But godliness with contentment is great gain. For we brought
nothing into the world, and we can take nothing out of it"
(1 Timothy 6:6-7)*

In 2015, Business Insider named Bill Gates the most generous person in the world, with a generosity index of 32-per-
cent and, at the time, lifetime donations equaling $27-billion.

But none of us know how Mr. Gates, or anyone else, scores
on a godliness index. It isn't even in our job description to take
a guess. God alone keeps the index and will reveal it only to that
person on the day of judgment. Romans 14:10b, "We will all
stand before God's judgment seat."

The truth is everyone, of any income, will be subject to the
same review. And they will be judged by the same standard: Jesus
Christ. The poorest will stand in line with the wealthiest. And
heaven won't allow any "cuts" or "quick check-ins."

Upward motion on the godliness index is propelled by the Holy Spirit. It's called resurrection power. Romans 8:11, "And if the Spirit of him who raised Jesus from the dead is living in you, he who raised Christ from the dead will also give life to your mortal bodies because of his Spirit who lives in you." He cares so much about your climb on the godliness index that He has committed Himself to you from now through eternity.

Gain without godliness can turn to emptiness. But gain with godliness can turn to completeness. The Bible says you are "complete in Him." You don't have to be acclaimed for your accomplishment to have a sense of purpose. Your earthly purpose is to keep a loose grip on the world and its stuff, and a tight grip on the eternal and its promises. Giving away to gain everything.

RELATED:

"Your relationship with God is the most important one in your life. And as with every relationship, it can only be cultivated through time." – Carla Sunberg

MY PRAYER:

Dear Jesus, being more like you in my values and commitments is the real goal of my life. Amen.

~~~~~~

62

REFRESH BY REFRESHING OTHERS

"One person gives freely, yet gains even more; another withholds unduly, but comes to poverty. A generous person will prosper; whoever refreshes others will be refreshed" (Proverbs 11:24-25)

For many, there is nothing quite like a glass of iced tea on a hot day. According to TeaUsa.com, on any given day, over 158-million Americans will be drinking tea. And over 85-percent of that tea will be iced. And, in the south, it will probably be sweetened. For some, drinking unsweetened tea is akin to eating bologna instead of turkey on Thanksgiving Day.

During our country's war for independence, tea was a precious commodity, a symbol of prosperity and political connections. And to share one's supply of tea was truly a generous act.

Serving a beverage to friends or strangers is one way to express your hospitality and concern. Jesus said, "If anyone gives even a cup of cold water to one of these little ones who is my disciple, truly I tell you, that person will certainly not lose their reward" (Matthew 10:42).

Any refreshment offered in the name of Jesus is refreshing. For example, bottled water has been a bridge of compassion to people who have been victims of disasters. By the untold millions of bottles, the distribution of water has brought relief to those left homeless or hurt.

Providing wells has been a lifesaver for people in undeveloped countries. And those donating funds or volunteering to build the wells usually come away as refreshed in spirit as those who have clean water are refreshed in body.

It's not about the project or product, however; it's about the response of those involved. Generosity drives generosity in a continuous chain of giving. And those who serve as links in that chain prosper both in soul and spirit.

RELATED:

"Stewardship begins with a lifestyle of abundance, generosity, and openness to others, and it leads to our open-handed management of all that God has given to us." – Craig Dunn

MY PRAYER:

Lord, thank You for the refreshing You have brought to my life when I have provided refreshment to others. Amen.

~~~~~~

6 3

BEGINNING AT HOME

"Anyone who does not provide for their relatives, and especially for their own household, has denied the faith and is worse than an unbeliever" (1 Timothy 5:8)

Every ten years, another national census record is made available to the public. But if you're looking for current results, you might be in for a wait. Census.gov says those records are confidential for 72 years to protect citizen privacy. For example, in 2012, the 1940 census records were released.

The booming interest in ancestry research says family and heritage are important. Census records provide someone's biographical information to the last detail. And those interested in their ancestry comb over the records for clues that will help them piece together their family of origin.

Family and heritage are also important in the Christian faith. The opening verse of the New Testament begins with these words: "This is the genealogy of Jesus the Messiah the son of David, the son of Abraham" (Matthew 1:1). The heritage of our spiritual family is traceable to the beginning of time, with each bio linked to the unfolding of biblical prophecy.

Biblical history is filled with family values. From the Garden of Eden to the Garden of Gethsemane, biological and spiritual families form the backdrop of God's redemption plan.

Paul gave Timothy, his spiritual son in the faith, lessons in both spiritual and biological family care. "Son, Christian service begins at home. Provide for your household."

It's true in our giving as well as in our living. We learn to give by giving to our family. Of course, that giving isn't always a monetary gift, but it's included. Children learn generosity from generous parents. And the view from our household windows can and should be a Christian worldview.

RELATED:

"Whatever you have learned or received or heard from me, or seen in me--put it into practice" (Philippians 4:9).

MY PRAYER:

Heavenly Father, strengthen me to follow You in such a way that those in my family will want to follow You. Amen.

~~~~~~~~~~~~~~~~~~~~~~~~~~~~~~~~~~~~~~

64

ON THE JERICHO ROAD

"Suppose a brother or a sister is without clothes and daily food.
If one of you says to them, 'Go in peace; keep warm and well fed,'
but does nothing about their physical needs, what good is it?"
(James 2:15-16)

Over $40-billion is spent on human service charities in America each year. Compare that with over $200-billion per year spent on entertainment, and our priorities become obvious. Caring and consumerism are often in a tug-of-war.

Our minds go back to that biblical scene on the Jericho Road, when a victim of assault and battery lay helpless, while others either stepped over him or went around him. Jesus used the parable to teach us about selfishness and selflessness. It was given during an exchange between Jesus and a "religious expert" who didn't know as much about true religion as he might have thought! "Who is my neighbor?"

The Master patiently answered him in the Good Samaritan story. The ugly side of it pointed out the representatives of religion and politics who detoured around the fallen man, on their way to what they thought were more important matters. The Samaritan nailed it when he stopped to help. The Scripture says "He took pity on him," bandaged his wounds, and found emergency housing for him. His parting words to the innkeeper, "Look after him . . . and when I return, I will reimburse you" (Luke 10:33-35).

Selfishness met its match in the actions of the least expected traveler on that road to Jericho. The Samaritan wasn't a bystander; he was a first responder. Our right living and giving must always have an outlet of both service and generosity.

RELATED:

"Giving to familiar causes and to folks we know is easy, but giving in unfamiliar circumstances to total strangers is a different matter, especially when that giving involves a bit of sacrifice." – Larry Moore

MY PRAYER:

Lord Jesus, give me a heart that sees the needs of others, and then, in compassion, may I give of my resources to meet those needs. Deal with any selfishness that may hinder the leading of Your Spirit in my life. Amen.

65

GREEDY INHERITANCE

"Be shepherds of God's flock that is under your care, watching
"over them—not because you must, but because you are willing,
as God wants you to be; not pursuing dishonest gain,
but eager to serve" (1 Peter 5:2)

Greed is something we inherited from our relatives. No, not our immediate relatives, or theirs; we got it from our first relatives: Adam and Eve. It races through the sinful nature we inherited from them, stealing joy from others and wrecking the best efforts of self. The Bible says "Don't be greedy, for a greedy person is an idolater, worshiping the things of this world" (Colossians 3:5b, NLT).

New Testament "shepherds of God's flock" (leaders) were specifically warned against dishonest gain. And that certainly included, but was not limited to, money. Coursing through our Adamic veins is a dormant tendency toward dishonest gain. It may include taking advantage of someone's physical, emotional, or vocational vulnerability, as much as taking advantage of their finances.

Scripture says greed must be "put to death" (Colossians 3:5a). In other words, surrender it to Christ. Let His generosity and sacrificial service take its place in you. Right living and right giving go hand in hand. Once we realize that everything we are, everything we have, and everything we do belongs to God, we can't be greedy with it. We gladly rejoice in what we can give to Him, and to others.

Christ-followers must be a people who "overbid" in generous service and sacrificial giving. Our pattern is the Cross, where Jesus paid the highest price to redeem the least deserving. "For God so loved . . . He gave." Filled with that kind of love, we are left without viable options.

RELATED:

"God hasn't distributed gifts and talents equally, and for that reason alone, we can be assured that our sense of self-worth isn't based on what we do. Our self-acceptance comes from our identity in Christ and our growth in Character." –Patsy Lewis

MY PRAYER:

Father, everything about You is loving and generous. May I be more like You in every way, every day. Amen.

MEET THE AUTHORS

CRAIG A. DUNN

After earning his Law Degree from Indiana University, Craig Dunn served in the development office at World Gospel Mission. Following that assignment, Craig served as the Assistant General Secretary and Legal Counsel for The Wesleyan Church. Craig currently serves as the Chief Executive Officer of Wesleyan Investment Foundation and Wesleyan Pension Fund.

LARRY MOORE

Larry Moore has served as an assistant pastor in the local church, as Director of Finance for the Wesleyan Pension Fund, and as the General Director of Stewardship Ministries for The Wesleyan Church. He currently serves as the Chief Operating Officer at Wesleyan Investment Foundation.

STAN TOLER

Stan Toler has served as a general superintendent in the Church of the Nazarene as well as a pastor for over 40 years in Ohio, Florida, Tennessee, and Oklahoma. He was elected general superintendent emeritus at the 2013 General Assembly in Indianapolis, Indiana. He has written over 100 books, including his best-sellers, God Has Never Failed Me, But He's Sure Scared Me to Death a Few Times; Practical Guide to Pastoral Ministry; his popular Minute Motivator series; Outstanding Leadership and his newest book, The Power of Your Attitude. His books have sold over 3 million copies.